Editor
Erica N. Russikoff, M.A.

Illustrator
Kelly McMahon

Cover Artist
Brenda DiAntonis

Editor in Chief
Karen J. Goldfluss, M.S. Ed.

Art Coordinator
Renée Christine Yates

Imaging
Rosa C. See

Author
Mary Rosenberg

Publisher
Mary D. Smith, M.S. Ed.

Correlations to the Common Core State Standards can be found at *http://www.teachercreated.com/standards/*.

Teacher Created Resources, Inc.
www.teachercreated.com
ISBN: 978-1-4206-3992-6

Reprinted, 2015
Made in U.S.A.

TABLE OF CONTENTS

Introduction

Welcome to Teacher Created Resources' *Daily Warm-Ups: Language Skills* for Grade 2. In the *Daily Warm-Ups* series, there are over 150 Warm-Ups that cover a wide range of writing skills: grammar, parts of speech, vocabulary, punctuation, and mechanics. Each Warm-Up provides a brief overview of a particular skill, an example of using the skill correctly, an activity for the skill, as well as a follow-up writing activity for applying the skill.

In the *Daily Warm-Ups* series, the Table of Contents, the McREL Language Arts Matrix, and the Tracking Sheet are all useful tools. The Table of Contents and the McREL Language Arts Matrix allow you to pinpoint specific skills for the student to work on. The McREL Language Arts Matrix shows the general skills that a student or child should know at each grade level. Additionally, the Tracking Sheet allows you and/or the student to keep track of his or her progress.

Daily Warm-Ups are ideal for both parents and teachers and are easy to use. For parents, select the skill you want to work on with your child, tear out the page, and preview the material with your child. Be sure to have your child note the topic that is being covered. This will allow your child to access the knowledge and information that he or she already knows about the skill. Continue to go over the page with your child, so the child will know what to do. When your child has completed the page, take a few minutes to correct the work and address any errors your child made. An easy-to-use answer key starts on page 161.

For the classroom teacher, simply identify the skill page that you want to use with the students and photocopy a class set. If several pages are available on a specific skill, you might want to photocopy the pages into individual packets for each student. When presenting the page to your students, start at the top of the page where it notes the topic (skill) that is being covered. By doing this, the students will begin to access the prior knowledge and information they already know about the topic. Immediately following the topic will be a brief definition of the topic. Have your students read it, so they can apply this knowledge in the Practice section. The Practice section has the student independently (or with guided practice) apply the skill. The final section, Write On!, provides a writing activity that incorporates that page's specific skill.

The skills covered in *Daily Warm-Ups: Language Skills* are skills that are used and needed every day. Help your children or students master these skills, as they will use these skills throughout the rest of their educational careers and lives.

STANDARDS CORRELATION

Each lesson in *Daily Warm-Ups: Language Skills* for Grade 2 meets one or more of the following language arts standards, which are used with permission from McREL. (Copyright 2009 McREL. Mid-continent Research for Education and Learning. 4601 DTC Boulevard, Suite 500, Denver, CO 80237. Telephone: 303-337-0990. Web site: *www.mcrel.org/standards-benchmarks.*) Visit *http://www.teachercreated.com/standards* for correlations to the Common Core State Standards.

Standard 1: Uses the general skills and strategies of the writing process

- Uses prewriting strategies to plan written work — Pages: 58–60
- Uses strategies to draft and revise written work — Pages: 58–59, 63, 66
- Uses strategies to edit and publish written work — Page: 66
- Uses strategies to organize written work — Pages: 58–60, 63
- Writes in a variety of forms or genres — Pages: 61–67

Standard 2: Uses the stylistic and rhetorical aspects of writing

- Uses declarative and interrogative sentences in written compositions — Pages: 43–48

Standard 3: Uses grammatical and mechanical conventions in written compositions

- Uses conventions of print in writing — Pages: 128–137
- Uses complete sentences in written compositions — Pages: 39–54, 63, 66
- Uses nouns in written compositions — Pages: 8–22
- Uses verbs in written compositions — Pages: 23–33
- Uses conventions of spelling in written compositions — Pages: 68–80, 151–153
- Uses conventions of capitalization in written compositions — Pages: 39–54, 128–145
- Uses conventions of punctuation in written compositions — Pages: 39–54, 115–127

Standard 4: Gathers and uses information for research purposes

- Uses a variety of sources to gather information — Pages: 58–60, 160

Standard 5: Uses the general skills and strategies of the reading process

- Uses basic elements of structural analysis to decode unknown words — Pages: 97–114, 125–127
- Understands level-appropriate sight words and vocabulary — Pages: 68–80

STANDARDS CORRELATION

Standard 7: Uses reading skills and strategies to understand and interpret a variety of informational texts

- Uses reading skills and strategies to understand informational texts — Pages: 146–160
- Relates new information to prior knowledge and experience — Pages: 58–60, 66

Standard 8: Uses listening and speaking strategies for different purposes

- Uses level-appropriate vocabulary in speech — Pages: 92–96

TRACKING SHEET

Parts of Speech		Parts of Speech *(cont.)*		Sentence Structure		Sentence Structure *(cont.)*		Vocabulary	
Page 8		Page 24		Page 39		Page 55		Page 68	
Page 9		Page 25		Page 40		Page 56		Page 69	
Page 10		Page 26		Page 41		Page 57		Page 70	
Page 11		Page 27		Page 42		Page 58		Page 71	
Page 12		Page 28		Page 43		Page 59		Page 72	
Page 13		Page 29		Page 44		Page 60		Page 73	
Page 14		Page 30		Page 45		Page 61		Page 74	
Page 15		Page 31		Page 46		Page 62		Page 75	
Page 16		Page 32		Page 47		Page 63		Page 76	
Page 17		Page 33		Page 48		Page 64		Page 77	
Page 18		Page 34		Page 49		Page 65		Page 78	
Page 19		Page 35		Page 50		Page 66		Page 79	
Page 20		Page 36		Page 51		Page 67		Page 80	
Page 21		Page 37		Page 52				Page 81	
Page 22		Page 38		Page 53				Page 82	
Page 23				Page 54				Page 83	

Vocabulary *(cont.)*		Vocabulary *(cont.)*		Punctuation		Mechanics and Usage		Reference Materials	
Page 84		Page 105		Page 115		Page 128		Page 146	
Page 85		Page 106		Page 116		Page 129		Page 147	
Page 86		Page 107		Page 117		Page 130		Page 148	
Page 87		Page 108		Page 118		Page 131		Page 149	
Page 88		Page 109		Page 119		Page 132		Page 150	
Page 89		Page 110		Page 120		Page 133		Page 151	
Page 90		Page 111		Page 121		Page 134		Page 152	
Page 91		Page 112		Page 122		Page 135		Page 153	
Page 92		Page 113		Page 123		Page 136		Page 154	
Page 93		Page 114		Page 124		Page 137		Page 155	
Page 94				Page 125		Page 138		Page 156	
Page 95				Page 126		Page 139		Page 157	
Page 96				Page 127		Page 140		Page 158	
Page 97						Page 141		Page 159	
Page 98						Page 142		Page 160	
Page 99						Page 143			
Page 100						Page 144			
Page 101						Page 145			
Page 102									
Page 103									
Page 104									

DAILY WARM-UPS

Name ______________________________ Date ____________

Nouns

A **noun** names a person, place, thing, or idea.

Examples: nurse, hospital, slippers, compassion

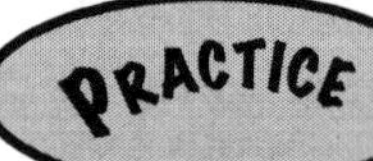

Write each noun in the correct category.

artist	yard	talent	studio
briefcase	power	lawyer	plant
paintbrush	gardener	office	joy

Person	Place	Thing	Idea
1.	1.	1.	1.
2.	2.	2.	2.
3.	3.	3.	3.

WRITE ON!

What do you want to be when you grow up? Write your response on a separate sheet of paper. Use nouns in the sentence, and underline them.

Name ____________________________ Date ____________

Declarative Sentences

There are four types of sentences: declarative, interrogative, imperative, and exclamatory. A **declarative sentence** is a telling sentence. A declarative sentence answers a question, gives information, or shares an opinion. A declarative sentence begins with a capital letter and ends with a period.

Example: Josh has a goldfish.

Circle the declarative, or telling, sentences.

Example: (The dog is getting a bath.)

1. Will you get in line?
2. We can play on the blacktop.
3. I brought a cold lunch.
4. I want to go play!
5. The children walk in a straight line.
6. The tennis shoes are new.
7. Write your name at the top of the paper.
8. Who knows the answer?

Write a declarative sentence about the picture.

____

____

On a separate sheet of paper, draw a picture. Write a declarative sentence about the picture.

Name ______________________ Date __________

Declarative Sentences

There are four types of sentences: declarative, interrogative, imperative, and exclamatory. A **declarative sentence** is a telling sentence. A declarative sentence answers a question, gives information, or shares an opinion. A declarative sentence begins with a capital letter and ends with a period.

Example: Keith grows cabbage in his garden.

Answer each question. Use a complete sentence.

Example: Do you like peanuts?
I love peanuts.

1. What is your favorite color?

____

____

2. When is your birthday?

____

____

3. Why do you like recess?

____

____

Draw a picture in the box of a pet you would like to have. Write a sentence about the pet.

____

____

On a separate sheet of paper, draw a picture of yourself as a baby. Write a sentence about the picture.

Name ______________________ Date __________

Declarative Sentences

There are four types of sentences: declarative, interrogative, imperative, and exclamatory. A **declarative sentence** is a telling sentence. A declarative sentence answers a question, gives information, or shares an opinion. A declarative sentence begins with a capital letter and ends with a period.

Example: Sabrina is left-handed.

Change the order of the words to make each question a statement.

Example: Did John throw a football?
John did throw a football.

1. Does Cassie play the violin?

   ____

2. Has Brent washed the car?

   ____

3. Is Jason feeding the dog?

   ____

4. Are they here?

   ____

Use a complete sentence to answer the question.

Is Carla painting a picture?

____

____

WRITE ON!

On a separate sheet of paper, draw a picture of a favorite hobby. Write two sentences about the picture.

Name ______________________________ Date __________

Interrogative Sentences

There are four types of sentences: declarative, interrogative, imperative, and exclamatory. An **interrogative sentence** asks a question. An interrogative sentence begins with a capital letter and ends with a question mark.

Example: What is your name?

Add a question mark to the sentences that ask a question.

Example: Does it rain in the desert?

1. Do you like to eat salad
2. My favorite actor is Kelly Carol
3. Don't lose the lunch money
4. Where are my car keys
5. When did Columbus discover America
6. Who likes doughnuts
7. We are watching Saturday morning cartoons
8. Did you find your homework

Write a question about the picture.

____

____

Write a question you would like to ask your teacher on a separate sheet of paper.

Name ______________________________ Date ____________

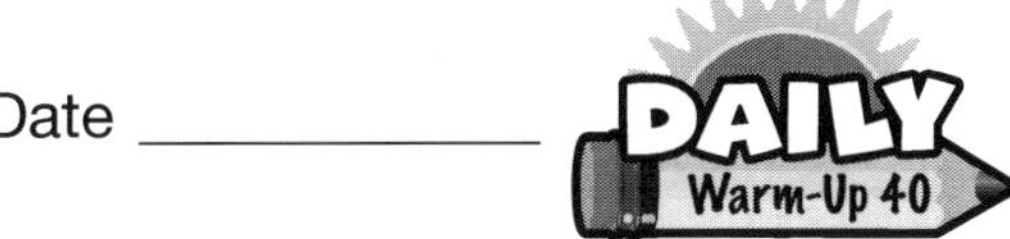

Interrogative Sentences

There are four types of sentences: declarative, interrogative, imperative, and exclamatory. An **interrogative sentence** asks a question. An interrogative sentence begins with a capital letter and ends with a question mark.

Example: When is winter vacation?

Change the order of the words to make each statement a question.

Example: Milo did walk the dog.
Did Milo walk the dog?

1. The telephone does ring at odd times.

____

2. Marcus can bowl a perfect game.

____

3. Wanda did get sick from eating candy.

____

4. The house was haunted.

____

Write a question about the picture.

____

____

WRITE ON!

On a separate sheet of paper, write two questions that you want to ask your mom or dad. Share the questions with your parent.

Name ______________________________ Date ____________

Interrogative Sentences

There are four types of sentences: declarative, interrogative, imperative, and exclamatory. An **interrogative sentence** asks a question. An interrogative sentence begins with a capital letter and ends with a question mark.

Example: Where did you get your jacket?

Write a question about each picture.

On a separate sheet of paper, write a question for a classmate to answer. Exchange papers with a classmate. Ask the classmate to answer the question.

Name ______________________________ Date ____________

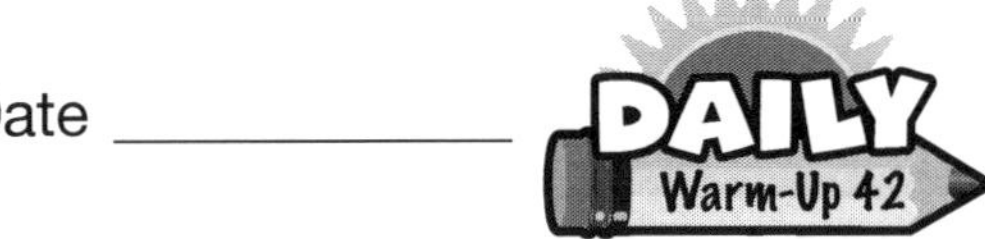

Imperative Sentences

There are four types of sentences: declarative, interrogative, imperative, and exclamatory. An **imperative sentence** is also known as a command. An imperative sentence gives an order. An imperative sentence begins with a capital letter and ends with a period. The subject of the sentence (*you*) is not usually used, but you know that the order is given to you.

Example: Clean your room.

Circle the imperative sentences.

Example: Pick the apples.

1. Pam loves to work.
2. Wash the dishes.
3. Cut your hair.
4. Vacuum the carpet.
5. Does Sally like pickles?
6. Stop talking.
7. Pack your bags.
8. Jamie had great test scores.
9. Brush your teeth.
10. Where is Lincoln, Nebraska?

Use an imperative sentence to tell what the parent is saying. Write it in the speech bubble.

WRITE ON!

Use imperative sentences to write three classroom rules on a separate sheet of paper.

Name ______________________ Date __________

Imperative Sentences

There are four types of sentences: declarative, interrogative, imperative, and exclamatory. An **imperative sentence is** also known as a command. An imperative sentence gives an order. An imperative sentence begins with a capital letter and ends with a period. The subject of the sentence (*you*) is not usually used, but you know that the order is given to you.

Example: Turn down the radio.

Rewrite each sentence as an imperative sentence.

Example: Will you feed the cat?
Feed the cat.

1. Mark does his homework.

   ____

2. Would you make your bed?

   ____

3. Jackie puts on a sweater when it is cold outside.

   ____

4. Opal always uses the crosswalk.

   ____

5. Mom wants Jenna to button her jacket.

   ____

6. Diana needs to cut her hair.

   ____

Write three imperative sentences that people should follow on a separate sheet of paper.

Name ____________________ Date ____________

Imperative Sentences

There are four types of sentences: declarative, interrogative, imperative, and exclamatory. An **imperative sentence** is also known as a command. An imperative sentence gives an order. An imperative sentence begins with a capital letter and ends with a period. The subject of the sentence (*you*) is not usually used, but you know that the order is given to you.

Example: Turn off the television.

Write an imperative sentence for each picture.

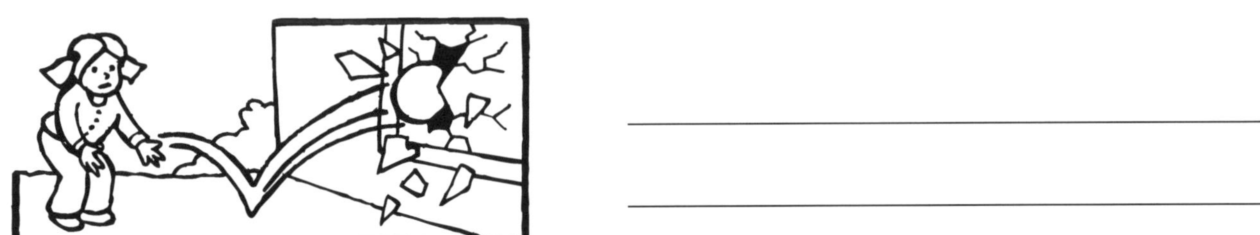

On a separate sheet of paper, write a declarative sentence. Rewrite the same sentence as an imperative sentence.

Name ______________________________ Date ____________

Exclamatory Sentences

There are four types of sentences: declarative, interrogative, imperative, and exclamatory. An **exclamatory sentence** shows strong emotion: anger, joy, happiness, excitement, and sadness. An exclamatory sentence begins with a capital letter and ends with an exclamation point.

Example: I just saw a giant rat!

Add an exclamation point to the sentences that show strong emotion.

Example: That movie was too scary!

1. I go to bed early on school nights
2. The plane almost hit my house
3. Does your dog bite
4. Dad caught a fish the size of a whale
5. We need to call 9-1-1
6. Which color do you like best
7. I can't believe he thought I was a famous actress

8. It is so hot

Write an exclamatory sentence about the picture.

____

____

Write a sentence on a separate sheet of paper. Rewrite the sentence to show strong emotion. Remember to use an exclamation point at the end of the sentence.

Name ______________________________ Date ____________

Exclamatory Sentences

There are four types of sentences: declarative, interrogative, imperative, and exclamatory. An **exclamatory sentence** shows strong emotion: anger, joy, happiness, excitement, and sadness. An exclamatory sentence begins with a capital letter and ends with an exclamation point.

Example: The alien took my pet hamster!

Read the paragraph. Circle the sentences that need an exclamation point.

Story #1

Jasper went to the awards show. He was up for an award for being the best new entertainer. Jasper couldn't believe it. He won.

Story #2

How exciting. Miles Shutterbug, the great photographer, is coming to our school. Miles is known for taking great pictures of people, animals, and trees. He is coming to our school as part of career day.

Write an exclamatory sentence about the picture.

____

____

On a separate sheet of paper, write an exclamatory sentence about an exciting event in your life. Share the sentence with a classmate.

Name ______________________________ Date ____________

Exclamatory Sentences

There are four types of sentences: declarative, interrogative, imperative, and exclamatory. An **exclamatory sentence** shows strong emotion: anger, joy, happiness, excitement, and sadness. An exclamatory sentence begins with a capital letter and ends with an exclamation point.

Example: There's a fly in my soup!

Write an exclamatory sentence about each picture.

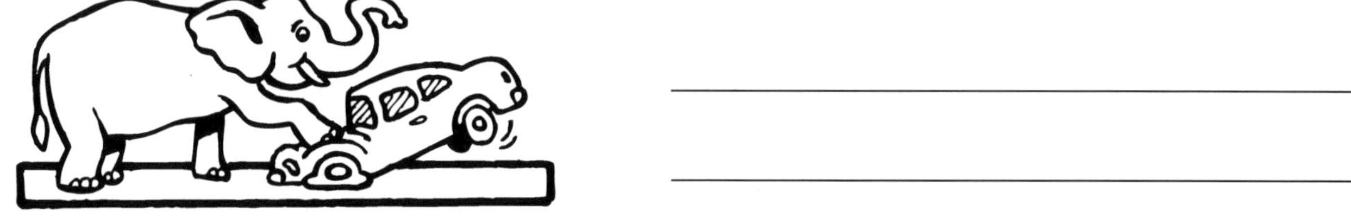

Write a sentence about something exciting you would like to do. Remember to use an exclamation point at the end of the sentence.

Name ______________________________ Date ____________

Sentence Types

There are four types of sentences: declarative, interrogative, imperative, and exclamatory.

- A **declarative sentence** is a telling sentence. A declarative sentence begins with a capital letter and ends with a period.
  Example: I can't find my calculator.
- An **interrogative sentence** is an asking sentence. An interrogative sentence begins with a capital letter and ends with a question mark.
  Example: Have you seen my calculator?
- An **imperative sentence** gives an order. An imperative sentence begins with a capital letter and ends with a period. The subject (*you*) is not usually used.
  Example: Find my calculator.
- An **exclamatory sentence** shows strong emotion. An exclamatory sentence begins with a capital letter and ends with an exclamation point.
  Example: I found my calculator!

PRACTICE

Identify each type of sentence.

D = Declarative **I** = Interrogative **IM** = Imperative **E** = Exclamatory

Example: I will see you at school. ___D___

1. How much was the ticket? ________
2. It was the best movie ever! ________
3. Who played Jack? ________
4. Tie your shoes. ________
5. The previews are starting. ________
6. There's the actor who played Sam! ________

Write a sentence on a separate sheet of paper. Exchange papers with a classmate. Ask the classmate to identify the type of sentence.

Name ______________________________ Date ____________

Correct Word Order

For a sentence to make sense, the words need to be in the **correct order**.

Example: found the student I.
I found the student.

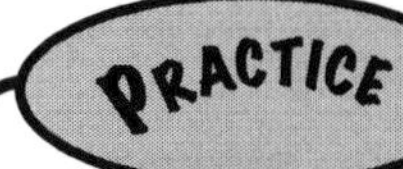

Read each pair of sentences. Circle the sentence with the correct word order.

Example: (I have a pet.)
a pet have I.

1. Where is Marvin?
   Is Marvin where?
2. Delicious the pancakes are.
   The pancakes are delicious.
3. Johnny loves to sing.
   Loves Johnny sing to.
4. Is the test when?
   When is the test?
5. Can you help me?
   Help can you me?
6. We played in the tree house.
   In the tree house played we.
7. Need you to your bed make.
   You need to make your bed.
8. The bakery is open.
   Is bakery the open.

On a separate sheet of paper, write a sentence with the words out of order. Exchange papers with a classmate. Ask the classmate to rewrite the sentence using the correct word order.

Name ______________________________ Date ____________

Correct Word Order

For a sentence to make sense, the words need to be in the **correct order**.

Example: good music the is.
The music is good.

Rewrite each sentence as a declarative sentence using the correct word order.

Example: scooter John new has a
John has a new scooter.

1. are the juicy apples

 ____

2. has pet Mr. Radford new a

 ____

3. makes spaghetti Molly wonderful

 ____

4. are the kids in pool the

 ____

5. help Kathleen needs

 ____

6. on the walked Daisy beach

 ____

On a separate sheet of paper, write a sentence with the words out of order. Exchange papers with a classmate. Ask the classmate to write the words in the correct word order.

Name ______________________________ Date ____________

DAILY Warm-Up 51

Compare and Contrast

When **comparing** two or more items, tell how the items are similar. Use words such as *both, similar, same,* and *alike.*

Example: Both the Chihuahua and Saint Bernard are dogs.

PRACTICE

Make a list telling how the house cat and tiger are **alike**.

	House Cat	**Tiger**
What type of animal is it?		
What does it look like?		
What does it eat?		

Write a paragraph telling how the house cat and tiger are the **same**.

House Cat and Tiger

____

____

____

____

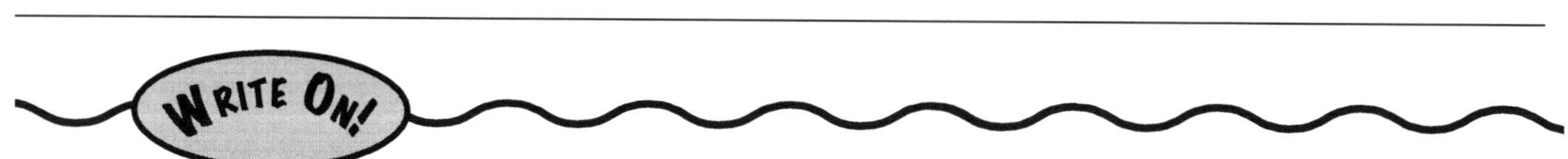

On a separate sheet of paper, write two sentences telling how you and a classmate are alike. Share the sentences with the classmate.

Name ______________________________ Date ____________

DAILY Warm-Up 52

Compare and Contrast

When **contrasting** two or more items, tell how the items are different. Use words such as *different, but, on the other hand,* and *although.*

Example: The Chihuahua is tiny, but the Saint Bernard is large.

PRACTICE

Make a list telling how the house cat and tiger are **different**.

	House Cat	Tiger
Where does the animal live?		
How does it get its food?		
How big is it?		

Write a paragraph telling how the house cat and tiger are **different**.

House Cat and Tiger

On a separate sheet of paper, write two sentences telling how you and a classmate are different. Share the sentences with the classmate.

Name ______________________________ Date ____________

Compare and Contrast

A Venn diagram can be used to tell how two things are **alike** and **different**.

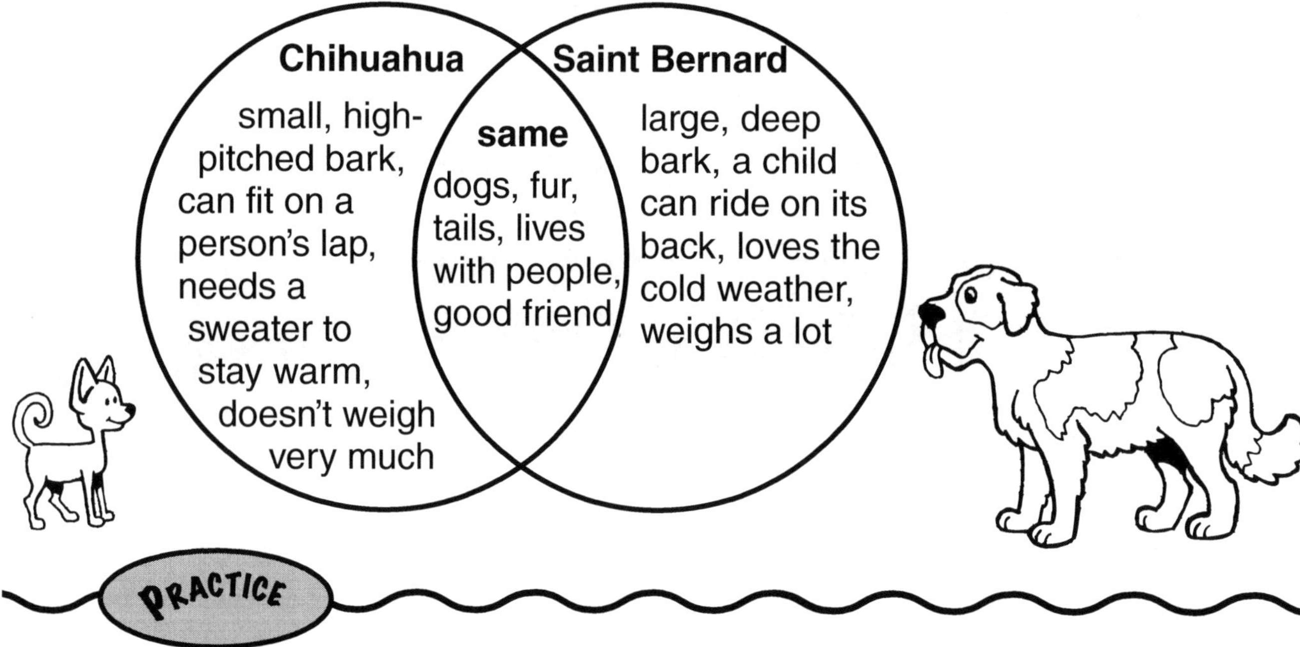

PRACTICE

Tell how a crib and a bed are the **same** and how they are **different**.

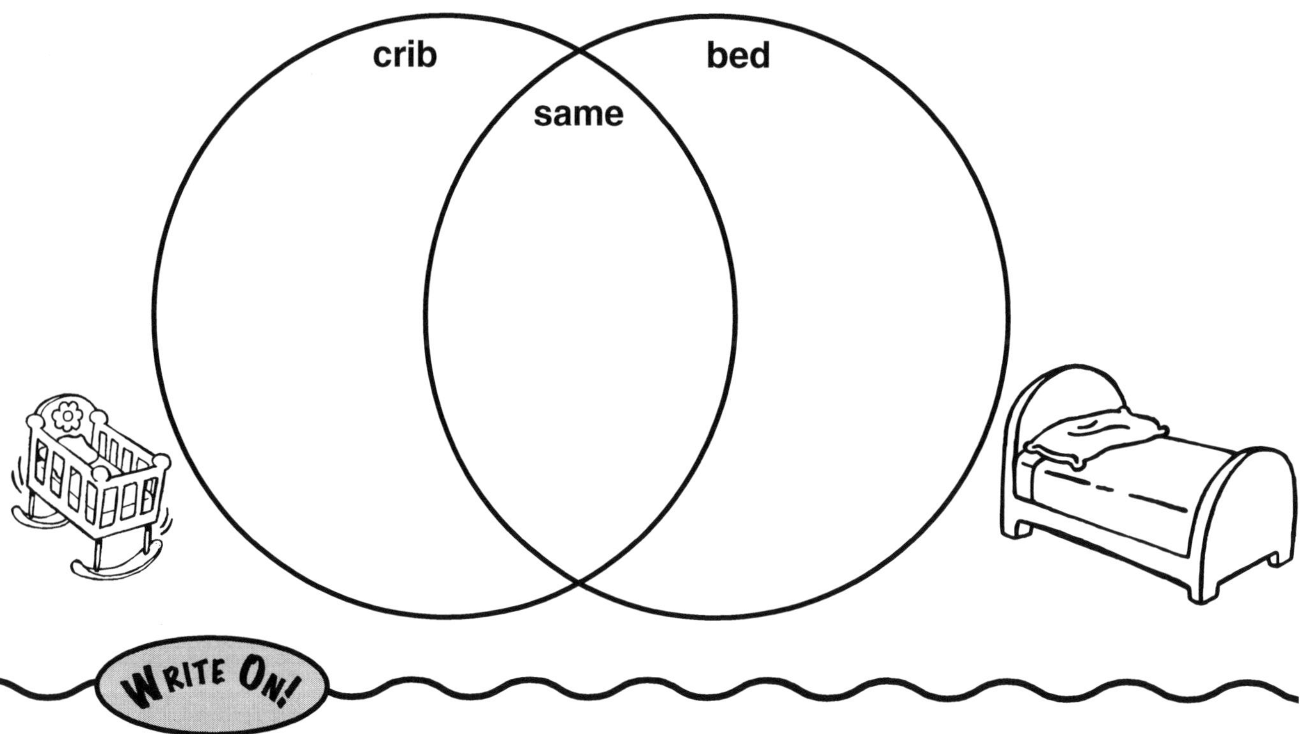

WRITE ON!

On a separate sheet of paper, write a paragraph comparing and contrasting a crib and a bed.

Name ______________________________ Date ____________

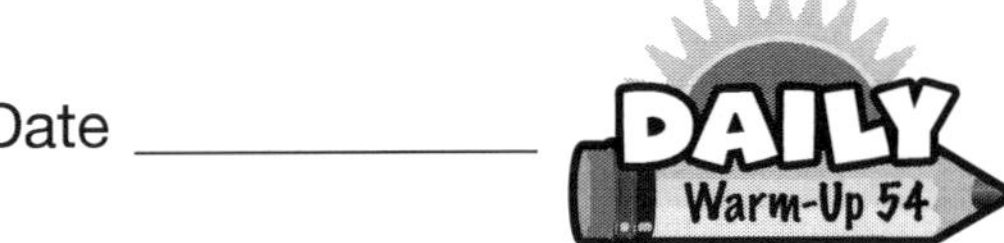

Writing a Friendly Letter

There are five parts to a **friendly letter**. The first part is the **date**. The date includes the month, the date, and the year. When writing the date, use a comma to separate the date from the year.

Example: March 28, 2008

Rewrite each date correctly.

Example: 23 October, 2008 ______October 23, 2008______

1. April, 15, 2005 ______________________
2. 5, 2008, June ______________________
3. August, 2009, 16 ______________________
4. February, 9 2000 ______________________
5. 2003, December 20 ______________________
6. 2007, 31, July ______________________
7. January 30 2001 ______________________
8. September 1 2004 ______________________

Write the following dates.

Today's date: ______________________

Your birthday: ______________________

A favorite holiday: ______________________

On a separate sheet of paper, write three dates with mistakes in them. Exchange papers with a classmate. Ask the classmate to rewrite each date correctly.

Name ______________________________ Date ____________

Writing a Friendly Letter

There are five parts to a **friendly letter**. The second part of a letter is the **greeting**. The greeting is a way of saying hello. The greeting is followed by the name of the person you are writing to. Use a comma after the person's name.

Example: Dear Mom,

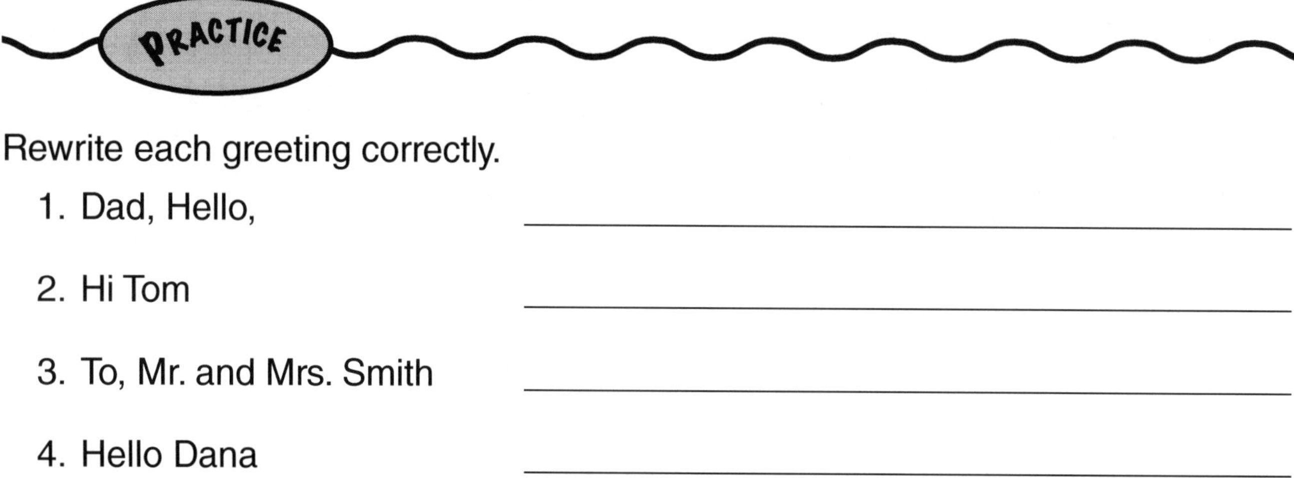

Rewrite each greeting correctly.

1. Dad, Hello, ______________________
2. Hi Tom ______________________
3. To, Mr. and Mrs. Smith ______________________
4. Hello Dana ______________________

Use the four words in the box below to write a greeting to a friend or family member. Remember to use a comma after the person's name.

Dear	Hello	Hi	To

Example: Hi Beth,

1. ______________________________
2. ______________________________
3. ______________________________
4. ______________________________

On a separate sheet of paper, make a list of other greetings that can be used to start a friendly letter. Share the list of greetings with the class.

Name ______________________ Date __________

Writing a Friendly Letter

There are five parts to a **friendly letter**. The third part of a friendly letter is the **body**. The body of the letter might ask a question or share information.

Example: How are you? I am fine. I have been busy learning multiplication and division facts.

Practice

Write three questions that you might ask someone in a letter.

1. ______________________
2. ______________________
3. ______________________

Write three statements that you might tell someone about yourself in a letter.

1. ______________________
2. ______________________
3. ______________________

Write On!

Write the body of a friendly letter to a classmate. Share what you wrote with the classmate.

____

____

____

____

Name ______________________________ Date ____________

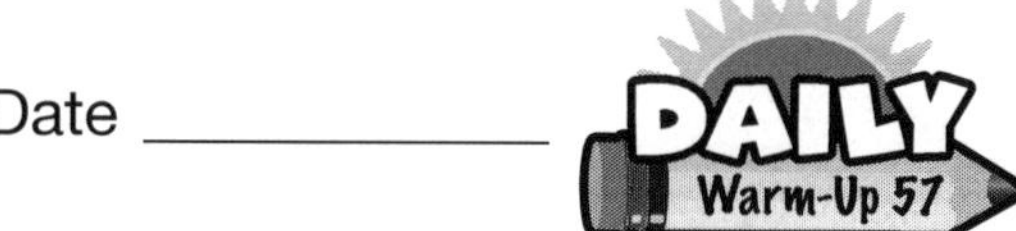

Writing a Friendly Letter

There are five parts to a **friendly letter**. The fourth and fifth parts of a friendly letter are the **closing** and the **signature**. The closing is a way of saying "good-bye." The closing begins with a capital letter and is followed by a comma. The signature is where you write your name.

Example: Your friend,
Seth

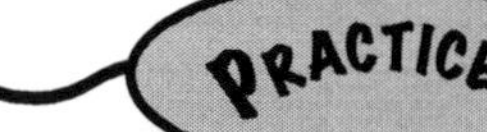

Rewrite each closing and signature correctly.

Example: yours truly Trish
Yours truly,
Trish

1. your best friend, Taylor

   ____

   ____

2. See you soon
   ana

   ____

   ____

3. hugs and kisses,
   Chad

   ____

   ____

4. Love always Reed

   ____

   ____

5. sincerely yours,
   tamra

   ____

   ____

6. love,
   arnie

   ____

   ____

On a separate sheet of paper, make a list of other words and phrases that can be used as closings. Share your list with the class.

Name ______________________ Date ____________

Writing a Friendly Letter

There are five parts to a **friendly letter**: the date, the greeting, the body of the letter, the closing, and the signature.

Identify each part of the friendly letter.

Body	Closing	Date	Greeting	Signature

A — November 1, 2008

Dear Grandma, — B

For Halloween, I dressed up as a giant carrot. Mom made the costume for me out of felt. She used orange felt for the body and green felt for the top of the carrot. I also wore orange leggings. That evening, I went trick-or-treating. Everyone agreed that I was the cutest vegetable they had ever seen!

— C

D — Love,

E — Nick

A. ______________________

B. ______________________

C. ______________________

D. ______________________

E. ______________________

On a separate sheet of paper, make a list of people you could write a friendly letter to. Select one person from the list, and send him or her a letter.

Name ______________________________ Date ____________

DAILY Warm-Up 59

Writing a Friendly Letter

There are five parts to a **friendly letter**: the date, the greeting, the body of the letter, the closing, and the signature.

PRACTICE

Write a friendly letter to a classmate. Remember to include all five parts in the letter: date, greeting, body, closing, and signature.

____
(date)

______________________,
(greeting)

____

____

____

____

____

____
(body)

______________________,
(closing)

____
(signature)

On a separate sheet of paper, rewrite the letter using a different greeting and closing.

Name ______________________________ Date ____________

DAILY Warm-Up 60

Writing a Friendly Letter

There are five parts to a **friendly letter**: the date, the greeting, the body of the letter, the closing, and the signature.

PRACTICE

Identify what is missing in each friendly letter.

Letter #1

October 1, 2008

We went swimming at Miller's Pond. The water was nice and cool. After swimming, we ate lunch under the trees. We had a great time.

Love,

Amy

What is missing? ______________________________

Letter #2

February 14, 2009

Dear Sue and Joe,

Your friend,

Sally

What is missing? ______________________________

On a separate sheet of paper, write a friendly letter, and be sure to leave off one of the parts of the letter. Exchange papers with a classmate. Have the classmate identify the missing part.

Name ______________________________ Date ____________

Spelling—CVC Pattern

Words that follow the **Consonant-Vowel-Consonant (CVC) pattern** have vowels that make the short sound.

Example: cat

Write the CVC word that goes with each picture.

1. ____________ 2. ____________ 3. ____________ 4. ____________

5. ____________ 6. ____________ 7. ____________ 8. ____________

On a separate sheet of paper, make a list of ten other CVC words. Draw a picture for each word.

Name ______________________________ Date ____________

Spelling—Digraphs

A **digraph** is when two letters work together to create a new sound. *Ch, sh, th,* and *wh* are digraphs. A digraph can be found at the beginning, in the middle, or at the end of a word.

Examples: thumb, pushes, sandwich

Write the word for each picture.

1. ____________ 2. ____________ 3. ____________ 4. ____________

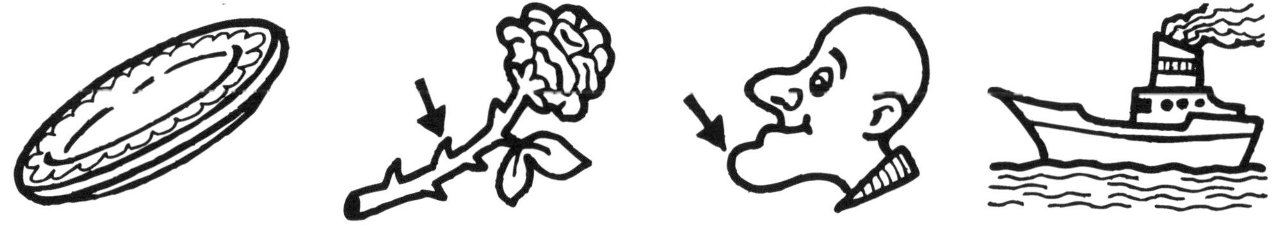

5. ____________ 6. ____________ 7. ____________ 8. ____________

On a separate sheet of paper, use two of the words in a sentence. Underline the digraph in each word.

Name ______________________ Date ____________

Spelling—CVCe Pattern

Words with the **Consonant-Vowel-Consonant-silent e spelling pattern** have a long vowel sound. The *e* is silent. It does not say anything.

Example: dime

Write the word on the line.

1. rob + e = ______________
2. mad + e = ______________
3. cop + e = ______________
4. mop + e = ______________
5. cap + e = ______________
6. pin + e = ______________
7. nap + e = ______________
8. mat + e = ______________
9. bit + e = ______________
10. tim + e = ______________
11. rat + e = ______________
12. pan + e = ______________

Circle the mistake in each sentence. Write the circled word correctly on the line.

Example: Jasper finally (mad) his bed. ____made____

1. The bubble gum machine takes only dims. ______________
2. How tall will a pin tree get? ______________
3. We decorated the tree with candy cans. ______________
4. I need a new tub of toothpaste. ______________
5. I have to take a not home to my parents. ______________
6. A lion has a great man of hair. ______________
7. Joanie is feeling fin today. ______________
8. I hop we can go to the museum, too. ______________

Use three of the CVCe words in a sentence on a separate sheet of paper. Underline the CVCe words.

Name ______________________________ Date ____________

Spelling—Vowel Pairs

A **vowel pair** is when two vowels are together in a word. The first vowel "does the talking and says its name."

Example: neat

The vowel pair is *ea*. The vowel pair makes the long *e* sound.

Write each word in the correct category.

neat	teen	feel	bean
meet	mean	seeds	steam

EA Words	EE Words
1. ______________	1. ______________
2. ______________	2. ______________
3. ______________	3. ______________
4. ______________	4. ______________

Complete each sentence using one of the words above.

1. Who ate the last jelly ______________ ?
2. Did you ______________ the new student?
3. Let's plant the ______________.
4. The giant is ______________.

On a separate sheet of paper, use two of the words in a sentence. Underline the vowel pair in each word.

Name ______________________________ Date ____________

Spelling—Consonant Blends

Two consonants together make a **consonant blend**. In a blend, each consonant's sound is heard.

Example: stone

Use the words below to complete each sentence.

slot	cramp	stand	clasp
belt	stop	soft	lost

1. Remember to ________________ by the grocery store.
2. Go ________________ in the corner.
3. Put the mail through the ________________.
4. Emily had a leg ________________ after running many miles.
5. Mickey got ________________ in the big store.
6. The ________________ on my necklace is broken.
7. The kitten has ________________ fur.
8. Who owns a black ________________?

Write two more words with consonant blends.

1. ______________________________
2. ______________________________

On a separate sheet of paper, use three of the words from above in a short story. Underline the words with consonant blends.

Name ______________________________ Date ____________

Spelling—Final /k/ Sound

The **final /k/ sound** can be spelled three different ways.

- Use a *–ck* if the /k/ sound follows a short vowel.
  Example: check
- Use a *–k* if the /k/ sound does not follow a short vowel.
  Example: bank
- Use *–ic* if the /k/ sound is in a multisyllable word.
  Example: picnic

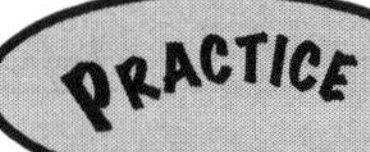

Write each word in the correct category.

ask	bunk	chunk	magic	magnetic
music	pack	park	plastic	peck
sack	sick	silk	sock	Titanic

–K Words	–CK Words	–IC Words
1. ________	1. ________	1. ________
2. ________	2. ________	2. ________
3. ________	3. ________	3. ________
4. ________	4. ________	4. ________
5. ________	5. ________	5. ________

On a separate sheet of paper, use two of the words from above in a sentence. Exchange papers with a classmate. Ask the classmate to underline the words that fit the rules.

Name ______________________________ Date __________

Spelling—Diphthongs

A **diphthong** is two letters blended together to make one vowel sound.

Example: /oi/ is a diphthong.
I will join the club.

Use the words below to complete each sentence.

oil	point	coin	noise
soil	voice	boil	foil

Example: Don't leave the food out too long, or it will spoil.

1. All plants need is ________________, air, water, and sunlight.
2. It's not polite to ________________ at others.
3. Keep the ________________ down, so we don't bother the neighbors.
4. This ________________ is called a peso, and it is used in Mexico.
5. Make sure you check the ________________ when you put gas in the car.
6. I lost my ________________ when I was sick.
7. Can you wrap the leftovers in ________________?
8. How long does it take to ________________ an egg?

On a separate sheet of paper, use three of the /oi/ words from above in one sentence. Share your sentence with a classmate.

Name ______________________ Date ____________

Spelling—Diphthongs

A **diphthong** is two letters blended together to make one vowel sound.

Example: /oy/ is a diphthong.
The holidays can be filled with joy.

Write the word that answers each riddle. Remember the word will have an /oy/ in it. If you need help, use a dictionary.

boy	destroy	enjoy	oyster	royal	voyage

Example: Something to play with. toy

1. Not a girl ____________
2. To wreck or ruin ____________
3. A creature that lives in the sea ____________
4. To go on a trip ____________
5. To like ____________
6. A king or queen is a member of this family ____________

WRITE ON!

On a separate sheet of paper, write about a favorite toy. Use words that have the /oy/ diphthong, and underline them.

Name ______________________ Date __________

Spelling—Diphthongs

A **diphthong** is two letters blended together to make one vowel sound.

Example: /ou/ is a diphthong.
A circle is round.

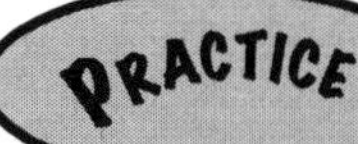

Use the words to complete each sentence.

cloud count found hour our outdoors

Example: Did you hear a sound?

1. ____________ family likes to play board games.
2. Which ____________ looks like a horse?
3. We have to play football ____________ .
4. Kitty ____________ her missing mittens.
5. Can you ____________ to one hundred?
6. We rode our bikes for an ____________ .

WRITE ON!

Describe a mountain on a separate sheet of paper. Use words that have the /ou/ diphthong, and underline them.

Name ______________________________ Date ____________

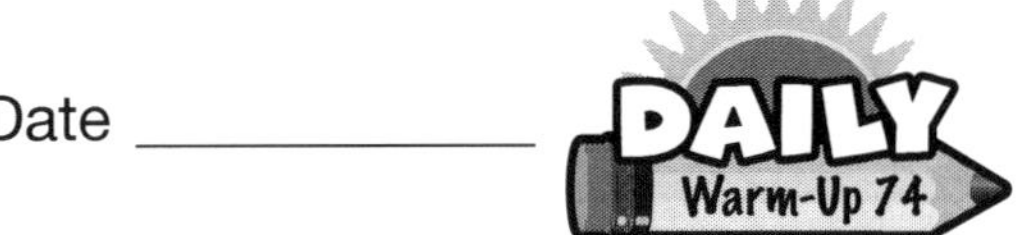

Homophones

Homophones are two or more words that sound the same but have different meanings and spellings.

Example: *Know* and *no* are homophones. They sound the same but have different meanings and spellings.

Know means to have information about something.

No means not allowed to do something.

- If you are not sure which word to use, try substituting *yes*. If *yes* makes sense, then *no* is the word to use. If *yes* does not make sense, then use *know*.
- Use *no* if giving a command or order.

Complete each sentence with the correct homophone—*know* (or *knows*) or *no*.

Example: I know how to tie my shoes.
("I yes how to tie my shoes" does not make any sense, so *know* is the word to use.)

1. Do you ______________ the way to San Jose?
2. ______________ way am I going to eat that bug!
3. Jim ______________ how to fix any type of computer.
4. There will be ______________ talking during the test.
5. Mr. Green ______________ my grandparents.
6. My mom always tells me ______________ .
7. Jalen ______________ how to play many sports.
8. I have ______________ idea where we are!

On a separate sheet of paper, use the words *know* and *no* in a short story. Share the story with a classmate.

Name ______________________________ Date ____________

Homophones

Homophones are two or more words that sound the same but have different meanings and spellings.

Example: *To, too,* and *two* are homophones. They sound the same but have different meanings and spellings.

- *Two* is a number word. If *three* (or any other number) makes sense in a sentence, then use *two*.
- *Too* means in addition to or in excess (over). If *also* or *over* makes sense in a sentence, then use *too*.
- *To* is a preposition. If *two* and *too* don't work, then this is the *to* to use!

Complete each sentence with the correct homophone—*to, too,* or *two.*

Example: I ate two whole pizzas!
("I ate three whole pizzas!" makes sense, so *two* is the word to use.)

1. I will give it ____________ you.
2. Maribel wants to go to the store, ____________.
3. Will you ____________ stop fighting?
4. Miles will take the books ____________ the library.
5. We would like a table for ____________.
6. During the holidays, people eat ____________ much food.
7. My dad bought a boat, life vests, and a boat trailer, ____________.
8. There are ____________ kids in the family.

How would you explain to someone when to use *to, too,* or *two*? Write your response on a separate sheet of paper.

Vocabulary

Name ______________________________ Date __________

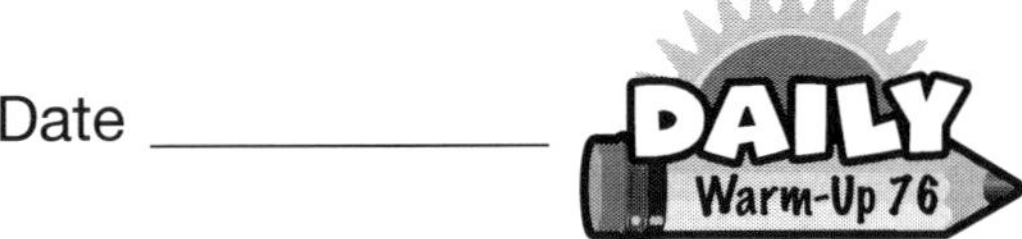

Homophones

Homophones are two or more words that sound the same but have different meanings and spellings.

Example: *Our, hour,* and *are* are homophones. They sound the same but have different meanings and spellings.

- *Our* shows ownership. If it makes sense to use *my*, then use *our*.
- *Are* is a helping verb. If it makes sense to use *were*, then use *are*.
- *Hour* is a measure of time. If it make sense to use *minute*, then use *hour*.

Complete each sentence with the correct homophone—*our, hour* (or *hours*), or *are*.

Example: The movie lasted three hours.
("The movie lasted three minutes" makes sense, so *hours* is the word to use.)

1. ____________ house has two stories and green trim.
2. We ____________ going camping this weekend.
3. How many ____________ does the program last?
4. This is ____________ favorite story.
5. It will take us an ____________ to reach the next town.
6. ____________ class is going on a field trip.
7. The zoo animals ____________ fed twice a day.
8. The cake needs to bake for an ____________.

On a separate sheet of paper, try to use all three homophones in the same sentence. Share your sentence with a classmate.

Name ______________________________________ Date ____________

Homophones

Homophones are two or more words that sound the same but have different meanings and spellings.

Example: *Ate* and *eight* are homophones. They sound the same but have different meanings and spellings.

- *Eight* is a number word. If another number word makes sense in the sentence, then use *eight*.
- *Ate* is a verb. It is the past tense of *eat*. If *eight* does not make sense in the sentence, then use *ate*.

Complete each sentence with the correct homophone—*ate* or *eight*.

Example: An octopus has eight legs.
("An octopus has seven legs" makes sense, so *eight* is the word to use.)

1. Who ______________ the last piece of pie?
2. The hotel is ______________ stories high.
3. Samantha is ______________ years old.
4. Are there ______________ days in one week?
5. The dog ______________ all of the crumbs on the floor.
6. There are ______________ people in my family.
7. Heidi ______________ lunch at the restaurant.
8. Jill ______________ twenty-three jelly beans.

Write the rules for using each homophone on a separate sheet of paper. Share the rules with a classmate.

Name ______________________________ Date ____________

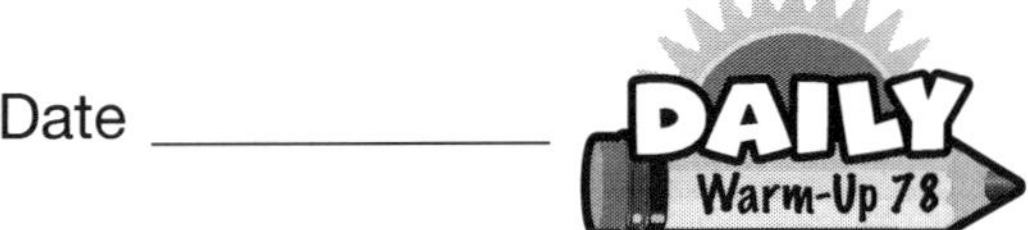

Homophones

Homophones are two or more words that sound the same but have different meanings and spellings.

Example: *There, their,* and *they're* are homophones. They sound the same but have different meanings and spellings.

- *There* tells a location. If *here* makes sense in the sentence, then *there* is the word to use.

  Example: I put the backpack over there.

- *Their* shows ownership. If *our* makes sense in the sentence, then *their* is the word to use.

  Example: Their car needs to be washed.

- *They're* is a contraction of *they are*. If *they are* makes sense in the sentence, then *they're* is the word to use.

  Example: They're always late!

Complete each sentence with the correct homophone—*there, their,* or *they're.*

Example: Their flight is due to land soon.

1. We have to walk the dogs over ____________ in the dog area.
2. Johnny left ____________ house and walked home.
3. ____________ getting ready for the carnival.
4. ____________ it is!
5. ____________ desserts are the best in town.
6. ____________ taking a spelling test.

On a separate sheet of paper, write a sentence using one of the homophones. Erase the homophone, and exchange papers with a classmate. Ask the classmate to write the correct homophone on the line.

Name ______________________________ Date __________

Word Confusion

A, an, and *and* often sound the same when spoken and are then misused when writing sentences.

A and *an* are articles. Articles are used before nouns. *A* and *an* mean "one" and are used with singular nouns.

- Use *a* if the next word begins with a consonant sound or the long *u* sound.
  Example: A unicorn is a horse with a horn.
- Use *an* if the next word begins with a vowel sound.
  Example: An apple a day keeps the doctor away.
- *And* is a conjunction. Use it when combining sentences or with a series of items.
  Example: I went fishing, and my brother went hunting.
  I can sing, dance, and clap my hands.

Complete each sentence with the correct word—*a, an,* or *and.*

Example: This piece of pie needs a scoop of ice cream!

1. Bugs are nasty, gross, ______________ dirty!
2. Do you want ______________ hamburger?
3. ______________ anteater really does eat ants.
4. Do you have ______________ cold?
5. Missy has ______________ earache.
6. My dog has ______________ collar.
7. Glen put sprinkles, cherries, nuts, ______________ hot fudge on his sundae.
8. Do you have ______________ minute?

On a separate sheet of paper, use the three words from above in a sentence. Share your sentence with a classmate.

Name ______________________________ Date ____________

Word Confusion

Much and *many* are used to describe nouns. *Much* and *many* mean "a lot of."

- Use *many* with plural nouns.
  Example: I have many friends.
- Use *much* with singular nouns.
  Example: I have much money.

Complete each sentence with the correct word—*much* or *many.*

Example: I have many things to do today.

1. Henry ate too ______________ food tonight.
2. Brandy has ______________ trading cards.
3. Harris has read ______________ books about dinosaurs.
4. Pat has traveled to ______________ other countries.
5. How ______________ did it cost?
6. Do you have ______________ homework tonight?

On a separate sheet of paper, write sentences using the words *much* and *many*. Underline the nouns that the words are describing.

Name ______________________________ Date ____________

Daily Warm-Up 81

Alliteration

Alliteration is when words begin with the same sound, but not always the same letter.

Examples: Allie Alligator always asks Annie for anything.
Cory's kite got stuck in the cactus.

Read the sentence. Underline the words and phrases that use alliteration.

Example: <u>Larry</u> <u>Lambert</u> is rarely <u>late</u> for work at his job at the <u>lab</u>.

1. The twins' eyes always twinkle when they see twine.
2. Marvelous Mary makes interesting maple pies using her mother's recipe.
3. Sally Summers sometimes sits in the sun smelling sunflowers.
4. Dean Davis and his dad, Derek, do double duty during the demolition derby.
5. Jay journeys by jet to visit his gerbil Jerome.
6. Bill's baby blanket barely covers his bed.
7. Kelly and her cousin Kim canned cucumbers and carrots.
8. Charles made chunky chocolate-chip cookies to cheer up his friend, Chuck.

For each word, write three other words that have the same beginning sound.

1. penny: ________________ , ________________ , ________________
2. nice: ________________ , ________________ , ________________
3. opal: ________________ , ________________ , ________________

Write a sentence using alliteration on a separate sheet of paper. Share the sentence with a classmate.

Name ________________________________ Date ____________

DAILY Warm-Up 82

Alliteration

Alliteration is when words begin with the same sound, but not always the same letter.

Example: Cindy Silver says that cities are simply sensational.

PRACTICE

Write the letters of your first name. For each letter, write three words that begin with the same sound.

Example:
B brave, beautiful, big
I into, imagination, igloo
L lovable, like, listen
L lucky, light, little
Y yes, you, yellow

____

____

____

____

____

Use the words to write alliterative sentences about yourself.

Example: Big Billy is a brave and beautiful boy. He likes listening to light music outside his impressive igloo.

____

____

____

Use the words you wrote to write a story about yourself on a separate sheet of paper.

Name ______________________________ Date ____________

Rhyming Words

Words with the same ending sound are **rhyming words.**

Example: stand, overhand, land

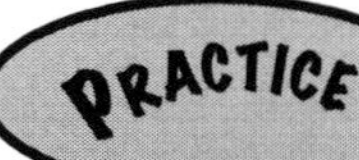

Circle the words that rhyme.

Example: (smile) (tile) (file) small

1. car	star	stir	scar
2. fancy	Nancy	antsy	pants
3. solar	parlor	polar	molar
4. hairy	hurry	fairy	Jerry
5. calf	laugh	ruff	half
6. head	sad	bed	fed
7. back	cake	rake	shake
8. pipe	dip	stripe	type

For each word, write three more rhyming words.

1. look: ____________________ , ____________________ , ____________________
2. tie: ____________________ , ____________________ , ____________________
3. hug: ____________________ , ____________________ , ____________________

On a separate sheet of paper, use three rhyming words in a sentence. Share your sentence with a classmate.

Example: I made a mile-high pie to share with Vi.

Name ______________________________ Date ____________

Rhyming Words

Words with the same ending sound are **rhyming words.**

Example: nose, rose, bows

Answer each riddle with a rhyming word.

banana	bear	bone	fault	late	puppy	wall	winner

1. Please give Hannah a big yellow ______________.
2. Be careful not to fall when skating down the brick ______________.
3. Somebody locked the vault. It wasn't my ______________.
4. The guppy won't grow up to be a ______________.
5. After dinner, we will pick a ______________.
6. If the dog answers the phone, he will get a juicy ______________.
7. Open the gate before it's too ______________.
8. I saw a hare chasing a ______________.

WRITE ON!

Write your own rhyming riddle on a separate sheet of paper. Share the riddle with a classmate.

Name ______________________________ Date ____________

DAILY Warm-Up 85

Synonyms

A **synonym** is a word that has the same or a similar meaning as another word.

Example: *Happy* and *glad* are synonyms.
Happy and *glad* have similar meanings.

Match each word to its synonym. If you need help, use a dictionary or thesaurus.

1. child	A. bonnet
2. eyeglasses	B. photograph
3. hat	C. pants
4. number	D. top
5. jeans	E. youngster
6. mutt	F. couch
7. picture	G. digit
8. shirt	H. plant
9. sofa	I. dog
10. tree	J. spectacles

Write a synonym for each word.

1. grin ____________________
2. instructor ____________________
3. classmate ____________________
4. vehicle ____________________

On a separate sheet of paper, use a pair of synonyms in a sentence.

Name ______________________________ Date ______________

Synonyms

A **synonym** is a word that has the same or a similar meaning as another word.

Example: *Sleepy* and *tired* are synonyms.
Sleepy and *tired* have similar meanings.

Underline the pair of synonyms in each sentence.

Example: If you need help, I can assist you.

1. When you make an error, erase the mistake and write the correct answer.
2. Add up the numbers to get the total.
3. The globe is a map of the world.
4. The tiny baby made a small cry.
5. The unmoving lion stood still in the grass.
6. This is her third try in her attempt to break the record.
7. Nathaniel hurts with pain.
8. The last person is at the end of the line.
9. The enormous elephant ate a large peanut.
10. John may help us, or he might not help us.
11. The noise is too loud.
12. The fresh coat of paint makes the room look new.
13. Do you see what I am looking at?
14. Listen carefully so that you hear all of the directions.

Write three words on a separate sheet of paper. Have a classmate write a synonym for each word.

Name ______________________________ Date ____________

Antonyms

An **antonym** is a word that has the opposite meaning of another word.

Example: *Day* and *night* are antonyms.
Day and *night* have opposite meanings.

Match each pair of antonyms.

1. brother	A. cat
2. closed	B. dad
3. dark	C. hate
4. dog	D. late
5. early	E. light
6. happy	F. off
7. love	G. open
8. mom	H. pepper
9. on	I. sad
10. salt	J. sister

Rewrite each sentence, replacing the underlined word with its antonym.

1. I <u>passed</u> the test!

____

2. Turn <u>down</u> the volume.

____

On a separate sheet of paper, use a pair of antonyms in a sentence. Illustrate the sentence.

Name ______________________ Date __________

Antonyms

An **antonym** is a word that has the opposite meaning of another word.

Example: *Full* and *empty* are antonyms.
Full and *empty* have opposite meanings.

Underline the pair of antonyms in each sentence.

Example: John needs to <u>level</u> the <u>uneven</u> ground.

1. The big horse belongs to my little brother.
2. After a hard day at work, Mom likes to sit in a soft chair.
3. When it's hot, Dad drinks cold water.
4. We drove over the hill and into the valley.
5. The roller coaster goes up and down.
6. At the swap meet, people can buy and sell things.
7. In my class there are nine boys and eleven girls.
8. Our parents like us to go together instead of alone.
9. Take the bent paper clip and straighten it out.
10. Eddie ate none of the vegetables and all of the desserts.
11. Sue repaired the broken window.
12. I need to clean my dirty room.
13. Can you walk on the line heel-to-toe?
14. That tiny dog has such a huge bark!

On a separate sheet of paper, write a sentence using a pair of antonyms. Share the sentence with a classmate.

Name ______________________________ Date __________

Synonyms and Antonyms

A **synonym** is a word that has the same or a similar meaning as another word.

Example: *Hard* and *difficult* are synonyms.

An **antonym** is a word that has the opposite meaning of another word.

Example: *Hard* and *easy* are antonyms.

Look at each pair of underlined words. Are they synonyms or antonyms? Write an **S** if you think it is a synonym, and write an **A** if you think it is an antonym.

Example: The glass is fragile.
The teacup is delicate. ___S___

1. The pupil studies hard.
   The student listens carefully. ______
2. Can you stand on your head?
   Put your shoes on your feet. ______
3. Hang your jacket on the hook.
   Put your coat on the hanger. ______
4. Carol has a beautiful voice.
   The crab is ugly. ______
5. George is starving.
   Isabelle is hungry. ______
6. James puts ketchup on hamburgers.
   Jane puts mustard on hot dogs. ______

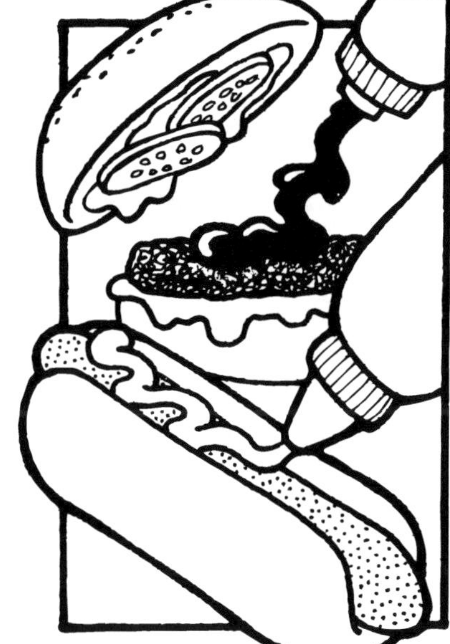

Write a pair of sentences on a separate sheet of paper. Underline one word in each sentence. Ask a classmate to write a synonym and an antonym for each word.

Name ____________________ Date __________

Compound Words

A **compound word** is made by combining two words into one unique word. The meaning of the compound word can be determined by looking at its two word parts.

Example: hairstylist
meaning: person who styles (does) hair

PRACTICE

Write the meaning for each compound word.

Example: wristwatch: a watch worn on the wrist

1. campfire: ____________________
2. buttermilk: ____________________
3. clothesline: ____________________
4. goldfish: ____________________
5. crosswalk: ____________________
6. shoelace: ____________________

Make three compound words.

cake	hay	pan	pig	stack	tail

1. ____________________
2. ____________________
3. ____________________

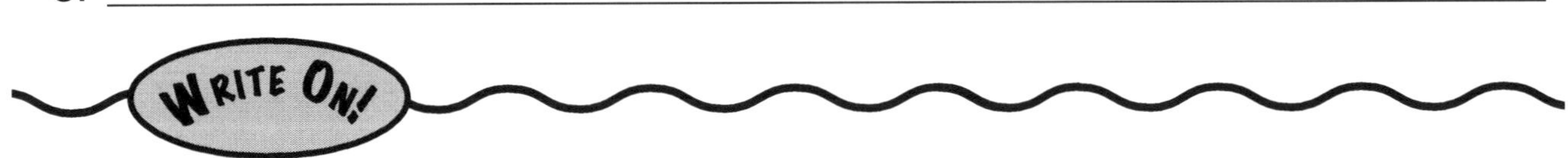

On a separate sheet of paper, use two of the compound words from above in a sentence.

Name ______________________________ Date ____________

Compound Words

A **compound word** is made by combining two words into one unique word. The meaning of the compound word can be determined by looking at its two word parts.

Example: sailboat

meaning: a boat that moves by using its sails

Write the compound word that answers each riddle.

cupcake	newspaper	rowboat	football
earthquake	eyeball	fireplace	skateboard

1. I'm a board with four wheels. Kids make me go by pushing with their feet. What am I? ________________
2. I'm a boat that moves with oars. What am I? ________________
3. I'm a little cake people eat on birthdays. What am I? ________________
4. You use me to see. What am I? ________________
5. People build fires in me. What am I? ________________
6. I make the ground shake and roll. What am I? ________________
7. Read me if you want to know what is happening today. What am I? ________________
8. I'm a ball that people kick with their feet and throw with their hands. What am I? ________________

On a separate sheet of paper, write a sentence explaining what a compound word is. Share your explanation with the class.

Name ______________________ Date ____________

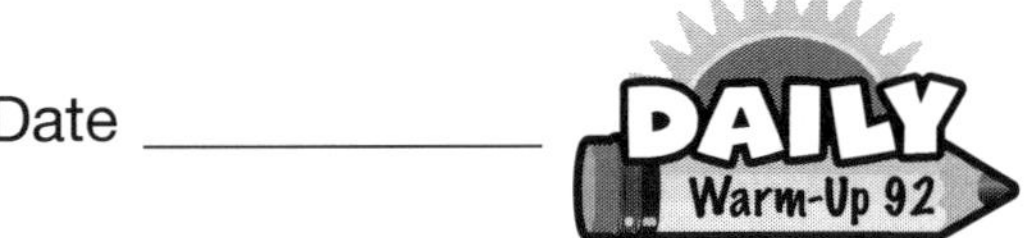

Compound Words

A **compound word** is made by combining two words into one unique word. The meaning of the compound word can be determined by looking at its two word parts.

Example: washcloth
meaning: a piece of cloth used for washing

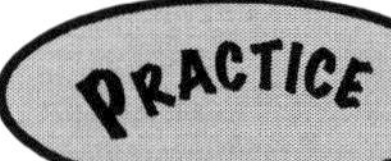

Make your own compound words using the list of words below.

air	door	man	room	steam
ball	grand	mother	shake	walk
board	hand	out	space	way

1. ______________________ 10. ______________________

2. ______________________ 11. ______________________

3. ______________________ 12. ______________________

4. ______________________ 13. ______________________

5. ______________________ 14. ______________________

6. ______________________ 15. ______________________

7. ______________________ 16. ______________________

8. ______________________ 17. ______________________

9. ______________________ 18. ______________________

On a separate sheet of paper, write about a visit to your grandparents. Use several compound words in the story, and underline them.

Name ______________________________ Date ____________

Compound Words

A **compound word** is made by combining two words into one unique word. The meaning of the compound word can be determined by looking at its two word parts.

Example: spacesuit
meaning: a suit worn in space

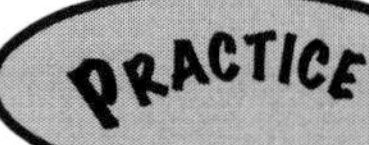

Circle the words that are compound words.

baggage	jacket	raincoat	tooth
bathrobe	lips	shoelace	turtleneck
bracelet	necklace	stocking	under
fingers	overalls	sweater	uniform
glasses	pajamas	swimsuit	wristwatch

Write each compound word and its meaning on the lines.

1. ____________________
2. ____________________
3. ____________________
4. ____________________
5. ____________________
6. ____________________
7. ____________________
8. ____________________

How is a compound word different from a regular word? Write your response on a separate sheet of paper.

Name ______________________________ Date ____________

DAILY Warm-Up 94

Syllables

All words have at least one syllable. A **syllable** is a sound segment within a given word. Each syllable must have a vowel in it. The vowels are *a, e, i, o, u* and sometimes *y*.

Examples: I (one-syllable word)
item (two-syllable word)
important (three-syllable word)

PRACTICE

Clap the syllables in each word. Write the number of syllables on the line.

Example: stapler 2

1. cup ______
2. picture ______
3. blanket ______
4. kitten ______
5. flat ______
6. lamp ______
7. frozen ______
8. number ______
9. telephone ______
10. pattern ______
11. desk ______
12. classroom ______
13. mail ______
14. playground ______
15. lollipop ______

Write a word with the number of syllables shown.

16. 1 syllable ______________________
17. 2 syllables ______________________
18. 3 syllables ______________________

WRITE ON!

Explain what a syllable is on a separate sheet of paper. Share your explanation with a classmate.

Vocabulary

Name ______________________ Date ____________

Syllabication Rules

All words have at least one syllable. A **syllable** is a sound segment within a given word. Each syllable must have a vowel in it. The vowels are *a, e, i, o, u* and sometimes *y*.

Examples: aim (one-syllable word)
after (two-syllable word)
already (three-syllable word)

For words with a vowel (long)-consonant-vowel pattern, divide the word between the first vowel and consonant.

Example: bro/ken

For words with a vowel (short)-consonant-vowel pattern, divide the word between the consonant and the second vowel.

Example: wag/on

Sort the words into long vowels and short vowels. Divide each word into its syllables. The first one has been done for you.

~~baby~~	denim	unite	river	navy	lizard
cabin	baker	photo	gravel	lemon	tiger

Long Vowels	Short Vowels
1. ba/by	1. ______
2. ______	2. ______
3. ______	3. ______
4. ______	4. ______
5. ______	5. ______
6. ______	6. ______

Write the two rules for dividing VCV words on a separate sheet of paper. Share the rules with a classmate.

Vocabulary

Name ______________________________ Date ____________

Syllabication Rules

All words have at least one syllable. A **syllable** is a sound segment within a given word. Each syllable must have a vowel in it. The vowels are *a, e, i, o, u* and sometimes *y.*

Examples: am (one-syllable word)
apple (two-syllable word)
avenue (three-syllable word)

For words that have a vowel-consonant-consonant-vowel pattern, divide the word between the two consonants.

Example: pup/py

Underline the VCCV pattern in each word. Divide the word into its syllables.

1. carton
2. mister
3. button
4. pattern
5. trumpet
6. bottom
7. picture
8. tennis
9. shallow
10. differ
11. ribbon
12. blanket
13. pizza
14. better
15. pillow
16. mirror
17. minnow
18. basket

Write two other words that fit the VCCV pattern.

1. ______________________________

2. ______________________________

On a separate sheet of paper, explain how to divide a VCCV word into its syllables. Share your explanation with the class.

Name ______________________________ Date ____________

Syllabication Rules

All words have at least one syllable. A **syllable** is a sound segment within a given word. Each syllable must have a vowel in it. The vowels are *a, e, i, o, u,* and sometimes *y*.

Examples: girl (one-syllable word)
enter (two-syllable word)
wonderful (three-syllable word)

For a vowel-consonant-consonant-consonant-vowel word, divide the word between the blend or the digraph and the other consonant.

Example: com/plete

Circle the correct way to divide each word into its syllables.

Example: district di/strict (dis/trict) dist/rict

1. explain	ex/plain	exp/lain	expl/ain
2. improve	impr/ove	imp/rove	im/prove
3. hundred	hundr/ed	hun/dred	hund/red
4. partner	part/ner	partn/er	par/tner
5. constant	co/nstant	con/stant	cons/tant
6. dolphin	do/lphin	dolph/in	dol/phin
7. employ	em/ploy	emp/loy	empl/oy
8. monster	mo/nster	mons/ter	mon/ster

Divide the following words into syllables.

1. English
2. hungry
3. distrust
4. portray
5. extra
6. pumpkin
7. instead
8. subtract

On a separate sheet of paper, explain the rules for dividing a VCCCV word into its syllables. Share the rules with a classmate.

Vocabulary

Name ______________________ Date ____________

Syllabication Rules

All words have at least one syllable. A **syllable** is a sound segment within a given word. Each syllable must have a vowel in it. The vowels are *a, e, i, o, u,* and sometimes *y*.

Examples: fast (one-syllable word)
never (two-syllable word)
lollipop (three-syllable word)

A compound word is always divided between its two word parts.

Example: corn/bread

Divide each compound word into its syllables.

Example: door/way

1. bathroom
2. Sunday
3. haircut
4. paintbrush
5. backpack
6. lighthouse
7. trashcan
8. into
9. rosebud
10. cupcake
11. pancake
12. sweatshirt
13. carwash
14. headache
15. peanut
16. hopscotch
17. eyeball
18. necklace
19. shoelace
20. flashlight

Write three compound words. Have a classmate divide each word into its syllables.

____________________, ____________________, ____________________

Name ______________________________ Date ____________

Syllabication Rules

All words have at least one syllable. A **syllable** is a sound segment within a given word. Each syllable must have a vowel in it. The vowels are *a, e, i, o, u,* and sometimes *y*.

Examples: bat (one-syllable word)
brownie (two-syllable word)
bakery (three-syllable word)

When a word has a prefix, divide the word between the prefix and the root word.

Example: return re/turn
re– is the prefix. *Turn* is the root word.

When a word has a suffix, divide the word between the root word and the suffix.

Example: turning turn/ing
Turn is the root word. *–ing* is the suffix.

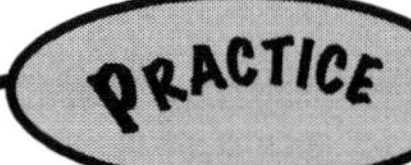

Sort the words into each category. Divide each word by its prefix or suffix and root word. The first one has been done for you.

friendly	teacher	meatless	subtitle	joyful
~~retell~~	playing	preheat	unlike	overeat

Prefixes	Suffixes
1. re/tell	1. ____________
2. ____________	2. ____________
3. ____________	3. ____________
4. ____________	4. ____________
5. ____________	5. ____________

On a separate sheet of paper, use two of the words from the word list in a sentence. Underline the words with prefixes and/or suffixes. Divide each word into its syllables.

Name ______________________________ Date ____________

Prefixes

A **prefix** is added to the beginning of a root or base word. A prefix changes the meaning of the root or base word.

Example: re + do = redo

re– is the prefix. It means repeat or again.

Do is the root or base word.

Redo means to do again.

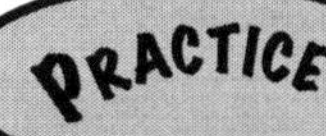

Add a prefix to each word.

dis = not **re** = repeat or again **un** = not

1. ___________ safe: to not be safe
2. ___________ like: to not like
3. ___________ tell: to tell again
4. ___________ able: not able
5. ___________ read: to read again
6. ___________ eaten: not eaten
7. ___________ order: not in order, messy
8. ___________ cover: to cover again

Use the words to complete each sentence.

Example: The old, rickety ladder is unsafe to climb on.

1. Ricky is ________________ to do the difficult work.
2. The shop will ________________ the old chair.
3. Harry and Terry ________________ eating liver and spinach.

On a separate sheet of paper, write three more words using the prefixes. Exchange papers with a classmate. Ask the classmate to write the meanings of the words.

Name ______________________________ Date ____________

Prefixes

A **prefix** is added to the beginning of a root or base word. A prefix changes the meaning of the root or base word.

Example: over + eat = overeat

over– is the prefix. It means too much. *Eat* is the root or base word.

Overeat means to eat too much.

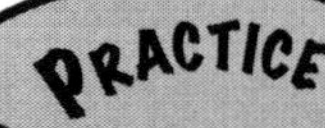

Match each word to its meaning.

over = too much, above **pre** = before **sub** = under, below

1. overpay	act too much
2. subzero	eat too much
3. preschool	pay too much
4. overeat	before the actual game
5. pregame	before kindergarten
6. subnormal	to wash before
7. overact	below normal
8. prewash	below zero

Use the words to complete the sentence.

1. I walk my little sister to her ____________________ each morning.
2. During the holidays, many people ____________________ .
3. Make sure you ____________________ the dirty dishes before putting them in the dishwasher.

WRITE ON!

On a separate sheet of paper, write about the holidays. What might you do too much of? Use words with prefixes in the paragraph, and underline them.

Name ______________________________ Date ____________

Suffixes

A **suffix** is added to the end of a base or root word. A suffix changes the meaning of the word.

Example: use + able = usable
Use is the base or root word.
–able is the suffix. It means having the ability to do something.
Useable means able to be used.

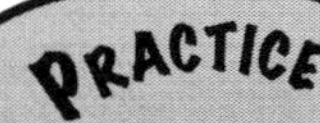

Read the base word and meaning. Then decide what the correct suffix is.

Example: joyful: full of joy

able = able to, ability to **er** = person or thing who is or does **ful** = full of

1. teach_____ : person who teaches
2. read_____: able to be read, legible
3. help_____ : providing plenty of help
4. wear_____ : able to be worn, suitable to be worn
5. swimm_____ : a person who swims
6. drink_____ : liquid that is safe to drink
7. use_____ : full of use, handy to have around
8. beauti_____ : full of beauty

Use the words to complete each sentence.

1. The character was a ___________________ princess.
2. Who is your second grade ___________________?
3. My dog loves the water and is a great ___________________.

On a separate sheet of paper, write three more words using the suffixes from above. Use one of the words in a sentence.

Name ______________________________ Date __________

Suffixes

A **suffix** is added to the end of a base or root word. A suffix changes the meaning of the word.

Example: talk + ing = talking
Talk is the base or root word.
–ing is the suffix. It means an ongoing action.
Talking means that someone continues to talk.

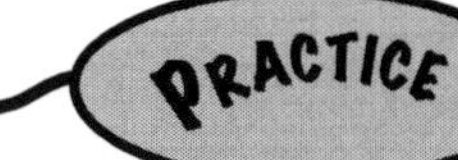

Make a list of words using the following base words + suffixes.

Base Words		Suffixes
friend	meat	*–ing* = ongoing action
help	slow	*–less* = without
hope		*–ly* = how something is done

1. ________________ 4. ________________ 7. ________________

2. ________________ 5. ________________ 8. ________________

3. ________________ 6. ________________ 9. ________________

Use the words to complete each sentence.

1. The vegetarian restaurant served ________________ lasagna.
2. The boy on crutches is ________________ down traffic.
3. Bea is a ________________ person.

On a separate sheet of paper, write about something you did to help others. Use words with suffixes in the story, and underline them.

Name ______________________________ Date ____________

Multiple-Meaning Words

Some words have more than one meaning.

Example: *Bed* is a multiple-meaning word.
Bed can be something a person sleeps in, or it can be a place in the yard for planting flowers.

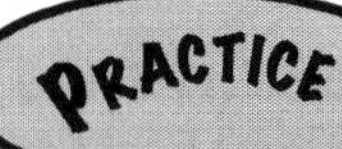

Match each word to its two meanings.

to fasten items together	box	the cresting water in the ocean
a sport with balls and pins	bowl	twelve inches in length
a student	can	a corn cob
a light rain	ear	a metal or aluminum container
a cube-shaped container	foot	an item worn around a man's neck
metal to fasten papers together	pupil	a sport
moving a hand back and forth	shower	a standard food item
to be able to	staple	a round dish
a body part	tie	used to clean oneself
something to hear with	wave	the inner part of one's eye

Use context (the other words in the sentence) to determine the meaning of the word. Write the meaning of the underlined word on the line.

1. I am a <u>pupil</u> at Rincon Elementary. ____________________
2. The light <u>shower</u> helped clean the air. ____________________
3. <u>Tie</u> your shoes before you trip over them! ____________________

On a separate sheet of paper, write a word with multiple meanings. Exchange papers with a classmate. Have the classmate write the two meanings of the word.

Vocabulary

Name ________________________________ Date ____________

Multiple-Meaning Words

Some words have more than one meaning.

Example: *Pet* is a multiple-meaning word.

Pet can mean an animal kept by a family, or it can mean to gently touch something.

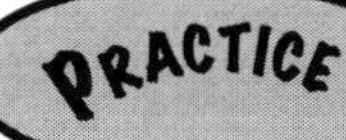

Write each word next to its pair of meanings.

baby	copy	cry	diamond	dress	eye	fall	fit	grade	land

1. ____________ : the year in school, points earned on a test or in a class
2. ____________ : to look at someone else's work, to make a replica
3. ____________ : to be in good shape, clothing of the right size
4. ____________ : a gem, a shape
5. ____________ : one of the four seasons of the year, to lose one's balance
6. ____________ : to put on one's clothes, a girl's article of clothing
7. ____________ : the ground, to bring a plane down from the air
8. ____________ : a yell, to weep
9. ____________ : an infant, the youngest member in the family
10. ____________ : a body part, the opening on a needle

On a separate sheet of paper, write the two meanings for one word. Exchange papers with a classmate. Have the classmate write the one word that fits both meanings.

Name ______________________________ Date ____________

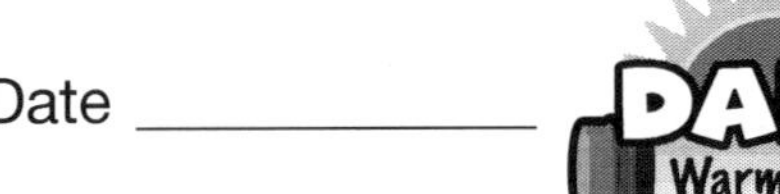

Multiple-Meaning Words

Some words have more than one meaning.

Example: *Wash* is a multiple-meaning word.
Wash can mean to do the laundry or to clean oneself.

Write the two meanings for each word.

Example: well: how a person might feel, a deep hole in the ground

1. king: ______________________________

____

2. rock: ______________________________

____

3. tag: ______________________________

____

4. batter: ______________________________

____

5. train: ______________________________

____

Write three more multiple-meaning words on a separate sheet of paper. Share the words with a classmate.

Name ______________________________ Date ____________

Multiple-Meaning Words

Some words have more than one meaning.

Example: *School* is a multiple-meaning word.
School can be a place of learning or a large group of fish.

The same word can be a noun—naming a person, place, thing, or idea, or a verb—describing an action. It depends upon how the word is being used in the sentence.

Example: Would you like a dinner roll? *Roll* is a noun.
Roll over. *Roll* is a verb.

PRACTICE

Identify the part of speech (*noun* or *verb*) for each multiple-meaning word.

Example: The children range in age from one year to ten years. ____verb____
The range is a vast open piece of land. ____noun____

1. The baby's rattle is pink and blue. ____________
2. Don't rattle the lion's cage. ____________
3. We will ship the packages tomorrow. ____________
4. The ship comes into port in the morning. ____________
5. The boys will model the new Boy Scout uniform. ____________
6. The model likes to walk down the runway. ____________
7. The punch tastes delicious. ____________
8. Do not punch your friends. ____________
9. I ride my bike very carefully. ____________
10. The ride was scary! ____________

What is the difference between a noun and a verb? How can this help in determining the meaning of a multiple-meaning word? Write your response on a separate sheet of paper.

Name ______________________________ Date ____________

Commas in a Series

A **comma** is used to separate three or more items in a list or series. The comma replaces all of the *ands* except for the last one.

Example: At the grocery store, I bought apples and bananas and cherries and dates and eggplant.

At the grocery store, I bought apples, bananas, cherries, dates, and eggplant.

Rewrite each list of words. Use commas to replace all of the *ands* except for the last one.

Example: When we went camping, we took tents and lanterns and sleeping bags and backpacks.

When we went camping, we took tents, lanterns, sleeping bags, and backpacks.

1. Thomas knows how to add and subtract and multiply and divide.

____

____

2. Michaela likes to collect toys and dolls and bears and rocks.

____

____

3. Gretchen planted roses and petunias and tulips and lilics.

____

____

4. Teddy packed pants and shorts and socks and belts.

____

____

On a separate sheet of paper, write a list of items you would buy from a store or take on a trip. Remember to use commas in place of *and*.

Name ______________________________ Date ____________

DAILY Warm-Up 109

Commas in a Series

A **comma** is used to separate three or more items in a list or series. The comma replaces all of the *ands* except for the last one.

Example: Pauline plays the piano and saxophone and tuba and clarinet.
Pauline plays the piano, saxophone, tuba, and clarinet.

PRACTICE

Rewrite the sentences, adding commas where they are needed.

Example: The dog ate my shoes and socks and belts.
The dog ate my shoes, socks, and belts.

1. Trisha has a television and radio and video games.

____

____

2. Leo drank his tea with lemon and sugar.

____

____

3. My sister has both eyeglasses and contacts.

____

____

4. Anissa was wearing earrings and bracelets and necklaces and rings.

____

____

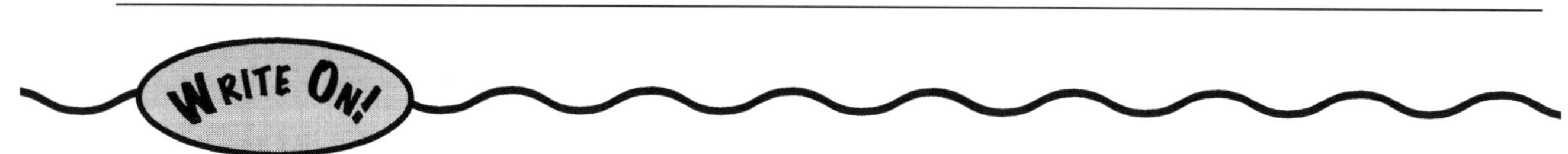

On a separate sheet of paper, write a list of more than two items. Then, write a sentence using the information in your list. Add commas where they are needed.

Name ______________________ Date ____________

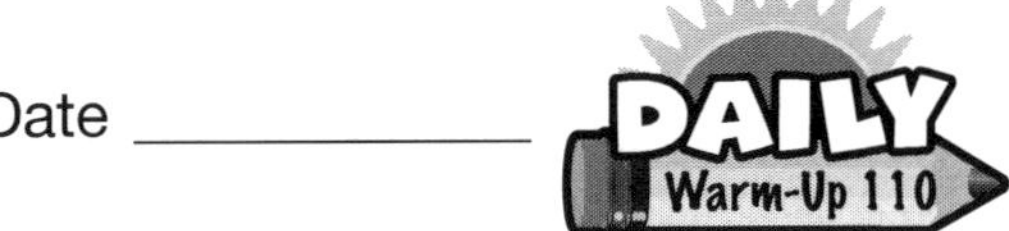

Commas in a Series

A **comma** is used to separate three or more items in a list or series. The comma replaces all of the *ands* except for the last one.

Example: I have soccer practice on Monday and Tuesday and Thursday and Friday.
I have soccer practice on Monday, Tuesday, Thursday, and Friday.

Read the paragraph. Place an **X** on the unnecessary *ands*, and replace them with commas.

Story #1

The class was planning a holiday party. The students wanted to have cupcakes and cookies and punch and party bags. The students would also need plates and cups and napkins. The students made a list of items and gave it to the teacher.

Story #2

Our school is great! Our school colors are red and white and black. Our school mascot is the lion. We have a football team and a softball team and a basketball team. We also have craft classes like painting and ceramics and photography and scrapbooking. You would love our school, too.

Story #3

We went to our grandparents' house for Thanksgiving. On the table was a lot of food. There were rolls and turkey and cranberry sauce and stuffing and potatoes. For dessert there were pies and cakes and candies and ice cream. We all ate until we were stuffed.

On a separate sheet of paper, write about an event that you have attended. Use a comma to separate the list of items that you saw or things that you did.

Name ______________________________ Date ____________

Quotation Marks

Use **quotation marks** to show someone's exact words.

Example: Mom said, "Come wash your hands."

No quotation marks are used if repeating what someone said.

Example: Mom said to wash your hands.

Draw a line under the person's exact words.

Example: Mrs. Simpson said, I think I will bake some cookies today.

1. I am going to use my grandma's secret recipe, whispered Mrs. Simpson.
2. Mrs. Simpson said that the cookies were done.
3. Yum! said Mr. Simpson.
4. The kids love Mrs. Simpson's cookies.
5. One time, Brett ate nine cookies.
6. Sally asked, May I have your recipe, Mrs. Simpson?
7. Certainly, said Mrs. Simpson.
8. The recipe is on the back of the bag.

On a separate sheet of paper, write a sentence using someone's exact words. Draw a line under the person's exact words.

Name ________________________________ Date ____________

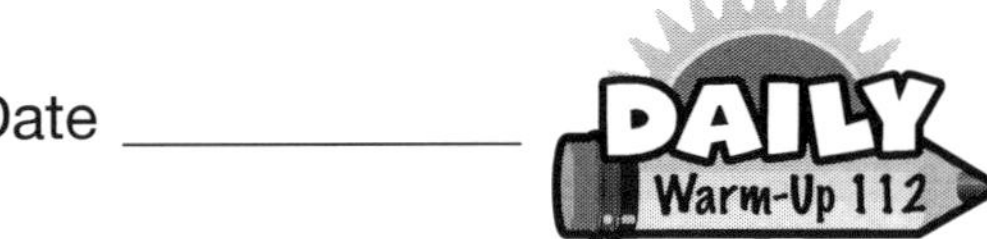

Quotation Marks

Use **quotation marks** to show someone's exact words. Capitalize the first word within the quotation marks. The punctuation marks go within the quotation marks.

Example: "I can't find my homework!" yelled Martha.

No quotation marks are used if repeating what someone said.

Example: Martha can't find her homework.

Put quotation marks around the person's exact words.

Example: Michael said, "I can do that."

1. Where do you live? asked Melissa.
2. I found my lucky penny! said Danny.
3. Caleb sighed, I forgot what I was going to say!
4. Gretchen asked, When is recess?
5. Wow! Look at that tall tree! said Simon.
6. Are Rich and Patrick twins? asked Trevor.
7. Cole wondered, Where did I put my soccer bag?
8. Can we go skiing this weekend? begged the kids.
9. Which shape do you like best? asked Mrs. Carlson.
10. My favorite season is fall, said Maribel.

Write a question and its answer on a separate sheet of paper. Use quotations marks around each person's exact words.

Example: Ivan asked, "Do you know what's for lunch?"
"No, I do not," said Steve.

Name ______________________________ Date ____________

Quotation Marks

Use **quotation marks** to show someone's exact words. Capitalize the first word within the quotation marks. The punctuation marks go within the quotation marks.

Example: "My missing mittens were underneath my bed!" yelled Preston.

If the person's words are interrupted, the second part of the quote does not begin with a capital letter.

Example: "My missing mittens," yelled Preston, "were underneath my bed!"

Use quotation marks around each person's exact words.

Example: "I like pretzels," said Marsha, "and potato chips, too."

1. When I get home, said Dad, we can go roller skating.
2. Well, the window was open, said the student, and a woodpecker came flying into the room.
3. Here comes the mail carrier, said Stewart, and she's carrying a big package!
4. In case of an emergency, said the police officer, remember to dial 9-1-1.

Correctly rewrite each sentence.

1. "what do you want to be when you grow up?" asked Samantha.

 ____

 ____

2. After school, said Elijah, let's go to the snack bar.

 ____

 ____

WRITE ON!

On a separate sheet of paper, write a sentence showing someone's exact words. Exchange papers with a classmate. Ask the classmate to add the quotation marks around the person's exact words.

Name ______________________________  Date ____________

Quotation Marks

Use **quotation marks** to show someone's exact words. Capitalize the first word within the quotation marks. The punctuation marks go within the quotation marks.

Example: "Can you help me?" asked Robert.

No quotation marks are used if repeating what someone said.

Example: Robert asked for help.

Read each paragraph. Add quotation marks around each person's exact words.

Paragraph #1

It's snowing! screamed Ralph. Let's make a snow family!

Okay! said Wanda. I'll grab carrots for the noses and some raisins for the eyes. The two kids ran outside and began rolling giant balls of snow. Soon the kids had made a whole family: a mom, a dad, a son, and a daughter.

They look great, said Wanda.

It was a lot of fun, said Ralph.

Paragraph #2

The next day, the sun came out and warmed the snow family.

Oh, no, sighed Wanda, the family is melting!

Don't worry, said Ralph, the next time it snows, we can make another family.

The kids watched as the snow family became a giant puddle. Soon the carrots and raisins were floating in the water. Wanda gathered up the carrots and raisins.

I will save these for the next family we make, said Wanda.

Good idea, said Ralph.

Write a dialogue (spoken words between two people) on a separate sheet of paper. Remember to use quotation marks around each person's exact words.

Name ______________________________ Date ______________

Possessives

An **apostrophe** is used to show ownership. When a noun is singular, add an apostrophe and an *–s* to show ownership.

Example: John has a hat.

Whose hat is it? John's hat

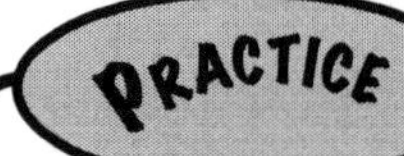

Decide who owns each item. Write your answer in the possessive form.

Example: This doll belongs to Susie. Susie's doll

1. Christian has an airplane. ______________
2. This jacket belongs to Gabriel. ______________
3. My brother has a backpack. ______________
4. Reanna has new eyeglasses. ______________
5. Mom has a red car. ______________
6. Sam made a movie. ______________
7. Audrey has long hair. ______________
8. Grandma has an antique lamp. ______________

Underline the possessive word in each sentence.

Example: <u>Mom's</u> cupcakes are the best!

1. Frank's house is built of brick.
2. The lamp's light is very bright.
3. My dog's collar is made of leather.
4. Have you seen Martin's baseball glove?

On a separate sheet of paper, write a sentence showing ownership. Use a possessive word in the sentence, and underline it.

Name ______________________________ Date ____________

Possessives

An **apostrophe** is used to show ownership.

Example: The president has a limousine.

Whose limousine is it? the president's limousine

Underline the possessives used in each story.

Story #1

My mom loves to quilt. She loves to go to her favorite fabric store, Stacy's Fabrics. While there, Mom looks through all of the fabrics. She finally picks the ones in her favorite colors: red, orange, and purple. Mom takes the fabric to the counter. The lady's sharp scissors cut quickly through the fabric. She puts Mom's fabric into a bag. Mom pays for the fabric at the counter.

Story #2

Dad's workshop is actually the garage. Out in his workshop, Dad makes all kinds of things. Dad's favorite project is to make toys for kids. Each year, Dad makes about a hundred toys to give to kids. The kids all love the toys and send Dad many nice letters. Dad hangs the kids' letters on a bulletin board in his workshop.

What does your friend's house look like? Use possessives in the sentences, and underline them.

____

____

Name ______________________________ Date ____________

Possessives

An **apostrophe** is used to show ownership. When a plural noun ends in –*s*, add an apostrophe to show ownership.

Example: The dogs' collars are brand new.

Dogs is plural. The apostrophe comes after the plural noun.

If a plural noun does not end in –*s*, add an apostrophe + –*s* to show ownership.

Example: The children's art work is hanging in the cafeteria.

Children is plural. The apostrophe + –*s* is added to show ownership.

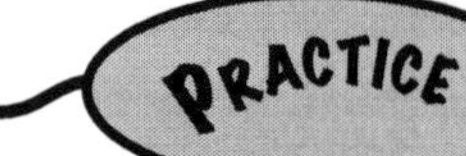

Decide who owns each item. Write your answer in the possessive form.

Example: The Simpsons have a new lawn mower. Simpsons' lawn mower

1. The soldiers shined their boots. ____________
2. The scouts wore their new uniforms. ____________
3. The flags had stripes in red and blue. ____________
4. The swans had white feathers. ____________
5. The cats clean their paws. ____________
6. The trees had delicious fruit. ____________

Underline the possessive word in each sentence.

1. The reporters' stories are on the nightly news.
2. The stores' sales are higher during the holidays.
3. The peacocks' feathers are very beautiful.
4. My brother ate the dogs' biscuits!
5. The students' portraits are hanging in the classroom.

On a separate sheet of paper, write a sentence using a plural possessive. Underline the possessive word.

Name ______________________________ Date ____________

Contractions

A **contraction** is made by combining two words into one shorter word. An apostrophe is used to take the place of the missing letters.

Example: should + not = shouldn't

Match each pair of words to its contraction.

1. I will	don't
2. he is	haven't
3. we are	he's
4. that is	I'm
5. you have	I'll
6. I am	isn't
7. do not	that's
8. will not	we're
9. have not	won't
10. is not	you've

Underline the two words that can be written as a contraction. Write the contraction on the line.

Example: I am hungry. ____I'm____

1. The car is not moving. ______________
2. Do not touch the wet paint. ______________
3. He is pushing the wagon. ______________
4. That is not a good idea. ______________

Write a sentence using a contraction on a separate sheet of paper. Underline the contraction.

Name ______________________ Date __________

Contractions

A **contraction** is made by combining two words into one shorter word. An apostrophe is used to take the place of the missing letters.

Example: would + not = wouldn't

Write the contraction for each pair of words.

1. you are __________
2. she is __________
3. it is __________
4. you will __________
5. they are __________
6. I have __________
7. will not __________
8. could not __________
9. she will __________
10. we are __________

Underline the contraction in each sentence. Write its two words on the line.

1. You're great at playing the piano. __________
2. He couldn't catch the football. __________
3. Ben isn't here. __________
4. It's time for the show to start. __________

WRITE ON!

On a separate sheet of paper, use a contraction in a sentence. Exchange papers with a classmate. Ask the classmate to underline the contraction and write its two words on the paper.

Name ______________________________ Date ____________

Contractions

A **contraction** is made by combining two words into one shorter word. An apostrophe is used to take the place of the missing letters.

Example: will + not = won't

Circle the contractions in the story. Then, write them below.

This month, I'm taking a class in woodworking. It's a fun class. I'll make all kinds of fun things. Today, I will make a wooden car. The wheels on the car are round. I've got sandpaper. The sandpaper will make the wheels smooth. Next, I use sandpaper to smooth out the rough edges on the car. I use wood glue to join all the pieces together. Then, I paint the car. I use special wood paint. The paint is really stinky, but once the paint is on, it looks beautiful. I can give the car to one of the kids in kindergarten. I think they'll like the car!

1. ____________________
2. ____________________
3. ____________________
4. ____________________
5. ____________________

Terry used an apostrophe in the following sentence: I have three brother's. Did Terry use the apostrophe correctly? Why? Write your response on a separate sheet of paper.

Name ______________________________ Date ____________

DAILY Warm-Up 121

Capital Letters

A proper noun names a specific person, place, or thing. A proper noun always begins with a **capital letter**.

Example: Mr. Kirby, the math teacher, drives a red car.

PRACTICE

Circle the proper noun in each example. Write the proper noun correctly on the line.

Example: mail carrier teacher (mikey) child <u>Mikey</u>

1. park roeding zoo aquarium forest

   ____

2. zippo sneakers sandals boots slippers

   ____

3. avenue street elm lane court

   ____

4. boy girl stella baby

   ____

Write a proper noun for each category.

1. Person: ______________________________
2. Place: ______________________________
3. Thing: ______________________________

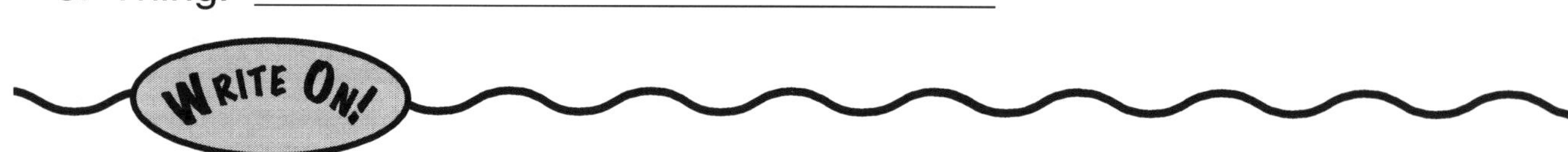

On a separate sheet of paper, use a proper noun in a sentence. Underline the proper noun.

Name ______________________________ Date ____________

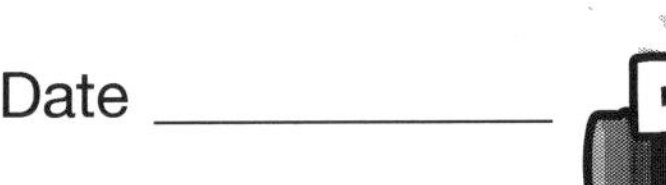

Capital Letters

A proper noun names a specific person, place, or thing. A proper noun always begins with a **capital letter**.

Example: Mrs. Leeds is in charge of the group.

Write each proper noun in the correct category.

Pancake Barn	Spot	Sandy Beach	Riley	Cube-It Blocks
Speedy Shoes	Dr. Morris	Puffy Bikes	Fresno Zoo	Shiny Shampoo
White House	Ms. Nolan	Mr. Simmons	Burger Time	Principal Rogers

Person	Place	Thing
1.	1.	1.
2.	2.	2.
3.	3.	3.
4.	4.	4.
5.	5.	5.

On a separate sheet of paper, write several sentences introducing yourself to a new student. Use proper nouns in the sentences, and underline them. Share your sentences with a classmate.

Name ______________________________ Date ____________

Capital Letters

All sentences begin with a **capital letter**.

Example: My house is red with white trim.

Draw three lines under the capital letter(s) in each sentence.

Example: I will buy a movie ticket.

1. When does the movie start?
2. Which theater is it playing in?
3. Would you like a tub of popcorn?
4. My sister works at the movie theater.
5. I love to watch movies.
6. I always watch the latest action movies.
7. My favorite character is Kung Fu Charlie.
8. He does the best stunts!
9. Do you like action movies, too?
10. Maybe we can go together sometime.

What kind of movie do you like best? Write about it on a separate sheet of paper. Draw three lines under the capital letter that begins each sentence.

Name ______________________________ Date ____________

Capital Letters

All sentences begin with a **capital letter**.

Example: Do you like to read fairy tales?

Rewrite each sentence using correct capital letters.

Example: we put the gear in the car.
We put the gear in the car.

1. my family and I go camping.

 ____

2. we take along tents and sleeping bags.

 ____

3. my mom packs the food.

 ____

4. my dad takes us on hikes.

 ____

5. my brother loves to canoe.

 ____

6. at night we roast marshmallows.

 ____

Would you like to go camping? Why? Write your response on a separate sheet of paper. Underline the capital letters that begin each sentence.

Name ______________________________ Date ____________

Capital Letters

All months of the year begin with a **capital letter**.

Example: January

PRACTICE

Write the name of each month using correct capital letters.

Example: october October

1. february ______________ 4. may ______________
2. june ______________ 5. september ______________
3. april ______________ 6. august ______________

Rewrite each sentence using correct capital letters.

Example: is february the shortest month of the year?
Is February the shortest month of the year?

1. Sara has a birthday in december.

____

2. in october, alice turns fifty-nine.

____

3. the final hockey game is in january.

____

4. were you born in march?

____

5. there are thirty-one days in july.

____

WRITE ON!

On a separate sheet of paper, write several sentences about the month in which you were born. Use proper nouns in the sentences, and underline them.

Name ______________________________ Date ____________

Capital Letters

All days of the week begin with a **capital letter**.

Example: Friday

Write each day of the week using correct capital letters.

Example: saturday Saturday

1. thursday ____________
2. wednesday ____________
3. tuesday ____________
4. monday ____________
5. sunday ____________
6. friday ____________

Rewrite each sentence using correct capital letters.

Example: harris has a hockey game on saturday.
Harris has a hockey game on Saturday.

1. i have a piano lesson on tuesday.

____

2. every friday night is family game night.

____

3. do you have karate practice on monday?

____

4. is the library open on wednesday?

____

On a separate sheet of paper, write about an activity you do on one of the days each week. Use proper nouns in the sentences, and underline them.

Name ______________________________ Date ____________

Capital Letters

A person's title, when used as a name, always begins with a **capital letter**.

Example: Dr. Thomas takes good care of his patients.

PRACTICE

Circle the sentences with titles used as part of a person's name.

Example: The governors meet every year.

Governor Smith is hosting the meeting.

1. The professors teach many classes.

   The math class is taught by Professor Manning.
2. Where is the detective?

   Where is Detective Johnson?
3. The nurse said that she would be right back.

   Nurse Adams is on the third floor.
4. Principal Hensel loves to work with children.

   Do you know where the principal is?

Rewrite each sentence using correct capital letters.

Example: coach clark is my neighbor.
Coach Clark is my neighbor.

1. I take my pets to see doctor warner.

   ____
2. judge holt is a very fair person.

   ____
3. mayor streets always keeps her word.

   ____

On a separate sheet of paper, write a sentence using a person's title and name. Underline the title and name used in the sentence.

Name ______________________________ Date ____________

Daily Warm-Up 128

Capital Letters

When writing a person's initials, always **capitalize** each letter, and use a period after each letter.

Example: J. J. Dumplings is my cousin.

Rewrite each sentence using correct capital letters and periods.

Example: My brother j.d. wants to be an animal trainer.
My brother J.D. wants to be an animal trainer.

1. My initials are mcr.

   ____

2. Have you eaten at cj's Barbecue?

   ____

3. mb threw the winning pitch.

   ____

4. You can call me Benny Bean or bb for short.

   ____

5. Uncle jr lives in Kansas.

   ____

6. My mom loves the poems by cc Edgemont.

   ____

On a separate sheet of paper, write a sentence using initials. Draw a line under the initials.

Name ______________________________ Date ____________

Capital Letters

When writing the name of a holiday, always use a **capital letter**.

Example: President's Day

Rewrite each holiday using correct capital letters.

1. hanukkah ______________
2. thanksgiving ______________
3. yom kippur ______________
4. ramadan ______________
5. mother's day ______________
6. new year's day ______________
7. christmas ______________
8. veteran's day ______________

Circle the mistakes in the paragraph. Then, rewrite the words correctly on the lines.

There are so many holidays each year. Some holidays honor people, and some holidays honor religious events. February is a busy month for holidays. groundhog day does not honor a person. It actually is a day to forecast how much longer winter will be around. After Groundhog Day, there is valentine's day. This is one of my favorite holidays. I love to make cards for all of my family and friends. Then there is lincoln's birthday and president's day. These days honor our past presidents. Which holiday do you like the best?

1. ______________________
2. ______________________
3. ______________________
4. ______________________

Write about your favorite holiday on a separate sheet of paper.

Name ________________________________ Date ____________

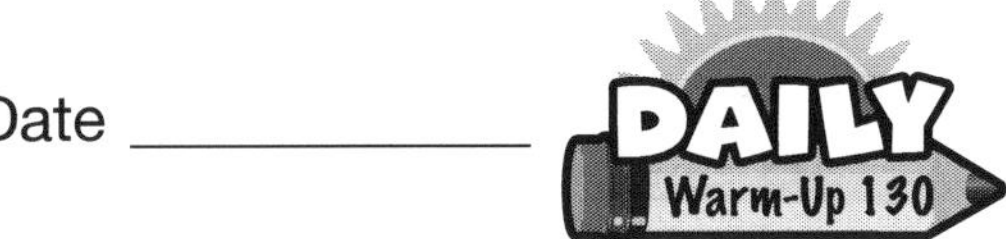

Capital Letters

When writing the title of a book or a movie, most words in the title begin with a **capital letter**. Short words, such as *a, to,* and *and* are not capitalized unless they begin a title. The title is also underlined.

Example: Matt went to see the latest action movie, The Great Hero of China and Beyond.

Underline the title in each sentence.

Example: Do you want to see The Flying Elephant?

1. The movie, Speedy to the Rescue, was a hit with kids of all ages.
2. Hannah is writing a book called Dancing Roses.
3. I can't find my copy of Even You Can Learn to Tap Dance anywhere.
4. Do you have a copy of the CD, Learn to Type in Ten Easy Lessons?
5. Camels Come to Dinner is one of the funniest movies of the year.
6. Tonight, The World's Funniest Videos is on at 8:00 p.m.
7. Bob and Peter are starring in Boys in Toyland.
8. The best-selling children's book is Cooking with Shmo and Joe.

Write the title of a favorite book. Remember to capitalize all of the important words and to underline the whole title.

____

Write the title of a favorite movie. Remember to capitalize all of the important words and to underline the whole title.

____

Write about a favorite book or movie on a separate sheet of paper. Remember to capitalize all of the important words in the title and to underline the whole title.

Name ______________________________ Date ____________

Abbreviations

An **abbreviation** is a shorter way of writing a longer word. When writing a person's title, the abbreviation begins with a capital letter and ends with a period.

Example: The abbreviation for *Mister* is Mr.

Match each word to its abbreviation.

1. Doctor	Capt.
2. Professor	Dr.
3. Sergeant	Jr.
4. Captain	Pres.
5. Junior	Prof.
6. Senior	Sgt.
7. Superintendent	Sr.
8. President	Supt.

Rewrite each sentence replacing the longer word with its abbreviation.

Example: President Tucker gave a long speech.
Pres. Tucker gave a long speech.

1. Fred Junior is named after his dad, Fred Senior.

____

2. Superintendent Jones runs the school district.

____

3. Captain Parisi has sailed ships for many years.

____

On a separate sheet of paper, write a sentence using an abbreviation in place of a person's title.

Mechanics and Usage

Name ______________________________ Date ____________

DAILY Warm-Up 132

Abbreviations

An **abbreviation** is a shorter way of writing a longer word. Most abbreviations for street or road signs begin with capital letters and end with periods.

Example: The abbreviation for *Boulevard* is Blvd.

Write the abbreviation for the street or road sign underlined in each sentence.

Ave.	E.	Ln.	N.	St.
Ct.	Hwy.	mi.	S.	Tpk.

Example: The population of Metropolis is 3,500 people. ___pop.___

1. The Red Rooster Restaurant is located off of Highway 99. ____________
2. Hanford Court has many restaurants and clothing stores. ____________
3. Red Bank Elementary School is on Avenue 8. ____________
4. We visited the candy shop on North Sweet Street. ____________
5. How many more miles until we get there? ____________
6. To get to the Capitol, turn left on State Street. ____________
7. My home is on Laurel Lane. ____________
8. Many trees are planted along East Elm Street. ____________
9. The cars that travel along the Tourist Turnpike pay a toll. ____________
10. We ride our skateboards at the South Street Park. ____________

On a separate sheet of paper, write the directions to get to your house, a park, or a neighborhood store. Share the directions with a classmate.

Name ______________________________ Date ____________

Abbreviations

An **abbreviation** is a shorter way of writing a longer word. For most states, the first two letters of the state's name are used in writing the abbreviation. There is no period after the abbreviation, and the letters are capitalized.

Example: The abbreviation for *California* is CA.

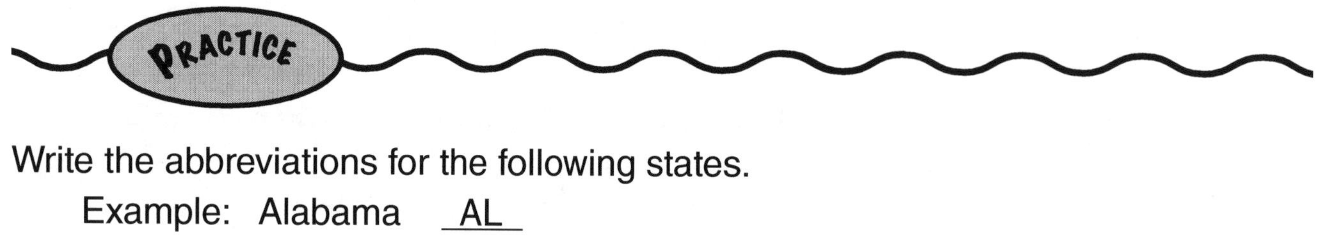

Write the abbreviations for the following states.

Example: Alabama AL

1. Arkansas ____________	9. Nebraska ____________
2. Colorado ____________	10. Ohio ____________
3. Delaware ____________	11. Oklahoma ____________
4. Florida ____________	12. Oregon ____________
5. Idaho ____________	13. Utah ____________
6. Illinois ____________	14. Washington ____________
7. Indiana ____________	15. Wisconsin ____________
8. Massachusetts ____________	16. Wyoming ____________

Use the state's abbreviation when addressing an envelope. Rewrite each address correctly.

Example: Exeter, California Exeter, CA

1. Seattle, Washington ____________
2. Boston, Massachusetts ____________
3. Orlando, Florida ____________
4. Denver, Colorado ____________

On a separate sheet of paper, write the two-letter abbreviation for your state and any neighboring states. Ask a classmate to write the name of each state next to its abbreviation.

Name ______________________________ Date ____________

Abbreviations

An **abbreviation** is a shorter way of writing a longer word.

For most states, the first two letters of the state's name are used in writing the abbreviation. There is no period after the abbreviation, and the letters are capitalized.

Example: The abbreviation for *Illinois* is IL.

Some states begin with the same two letters. To avoid confusion, those states use the first letter and a different letter in their abbreviations.

Example: Alabama and Alaska both begin with "Al."
The abbreviation for *Alabama* is AL.
The abbreviation for *Alaska* is AK.

Match each state's name to its abbreviation.

1. Arizona	HI
2. Connecticut	KY
3. Georgia	NV
4. Hawaii	TX
5. Kansas	GA
6. Kentucky	LA
7. Louisiana	AZ
8. Maine	KS
9. Maryland	MT
10. Montana	ME
11. Nevada	CT
12. Tennessee	TN
13. Texas	VT
14. Vermont	VA
15. Virginia	MD

What other way could states with the same beginning letters be abbreviated? Write your response on a separate sheet of paper.

Name ______________________________ Date __________

DAILY Warm-Up 135

Abbreviations

An **abbreviation** is a shorter way of writing a longer word. For most states, the first two letters of the state's name are used in writing the abbreviation. There is no period after the abbreviation, and the letters are capitalized.

Example: The abbreviation for *Michigan* is MI.

Some states have two parts in their names. Their abbreviations are the first letter in each part of their names.

Example: The abbreviation for *New Mexico* is NM.

PRACTICE

Write the abbreviations for the following states.

Example: New Hampshire NH

1. New Jersey ________
2. New York ________
3. North Carolina ________
4. North Dakota ________
5. Rhode Island ________
6. South Carolina ________
7. South Dakota ________
8. West Virginia ________

Circle the names of the states in the paragraph below.

Grandma and Grandpa love to see the fall colors. Each year, they travel from New Mexico to New Hampshire. From there, my grandparents travel along the East Coast to North Carolina, South Carolina, and West Virginia. My grandparents then fly to Rhode Island to visit my Uncle Rob.

Write the abbreviations for the states used in the paragraph.

1. __________
2. __________
3. __________
4. __________
5. __________
6. __________

WRITE ON!

Which is quicker to read, the state's name or its abbreviation? Why? Write your response on a separate sheet of paper.

Name ______________________________ Date ____________

Abbreviations

An **abbreviation** is a shorter way of writing a longer word. For days of the week, use the first three or four letters in the day's name. Begin the abbreviation with a capital letter and end it with a period.

Example: The abbreviation for *Sunday* is Sun.

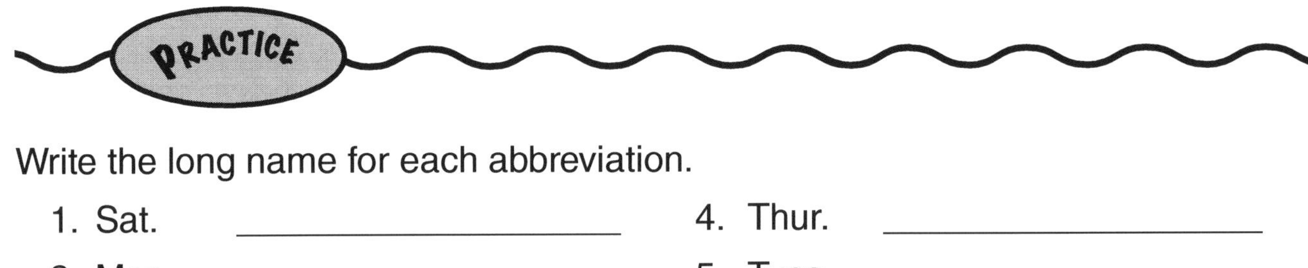

Write the long name for each abbreviation.

1. Sat. ____________________
2. Mon. ____________________
3. Fri. ____________________
4. Thur. ____________________
5. Tues. ____________________
6. Wed. ____________________

Circle the days of the week in the paragraph.

Maya is very busy. Each day of the week she has a different activity. On Monday and Wednesday, Maya takes a crafts class. She gets to make different projects using craft sticks, cotton balls, yarn, and clay. On Tuesday, Maya has piano lessons. Her teacher is Mrs. Mansfield. On Thursday and Saturday, Maya has soccer practice, and then she plays a game on Sunday afternoon. Friday night is family night. Maya and her family play board games together.

Write the abbreviation for each circled day of the week.

1. ____________________
2. ____________________
3. ____________________
4. ____________________
5. ____________________
6. ____________________
7. ____________________

What do you do each week? Write about your activities on a separate sheet of paper. Circle the days of the week that can be abbreviated.

Name ______________________________ Date ____________

DAILY Warm-Up 137

Abbreviations

An **abbreviation** is a shorter way of writing a longer word. To write the abbreviations for the months of the year, use the first three letters in the name of the month. In the case of September, you will use the first four letters in the name of the month. Begin the abbreviation with a capital letter and end it with a period.

Example: The abbreviation for *January* is Jan.

For months with only three or four letters, no abbreviation is needed.

Example: May is the fifth month of the year.

PRACTICE

Write the abbreviations for each month of the year.

Example: December <u>Dec.</u>

1. October __________
2. March __________
3. February __________
4. May __________
5. April __________

Use abbreviations to answer each question.

1. What is the month of your birthday? ______________
2. What is your favorite month of the year? ______________
3. What is the month the school year begins? ______________
4. What is the month the school year ends? ______________
5. Name a summer month. ______________
6. Name a winter month. ______________
7. Name a fall month. ______________
8. Name a spring month. ______________

On a separate sheet of paper, write about your favorite month of the year. What makes that month so special? What do you do during that month? Share your story with the class.

Name ______________________ Date __________

Abbreviations

An **abbreviation** is a shorter way of writing a longer word. For abbreviations for U.S. weights and measures, use lowercase letters and periods.

Example: The abbreviation for *inch* is in.

U.S. Weights and Measures			
foot/feet = ft.	pint = pt.	cup = c.	gallon = gal.
yard = yd.	quart = qt.	tablespoon = tbsp.	pound = lb.
mile = mi.	ounce = oz.	teaspoon = tsp.	

Underline the weight or measure used in each sentence. Write its abbreviation on the line.

Example: The carpenter cut the board to 3 feet in length. ft.

1. How many tablespoons of butter does the recipe call for? ________
2. We traveled two hundred miles to get to the beach. ________
3. The coffee pot holds eight cups of coffee. ________
4. The box of candy weighed 12 ounces. ________
5. Herbie drank a quart of chocolate milk. ________
6. How long is one yard? ________
7. Mom likes two teaspoons of cream in her coffee. ________
8. We get half a pint of milk with our snack. ________
9. The doctor said that I lost 1 pound. ________
10. How much does a gallon of gas cost? ________

What types of measurement tools have you used and why? Write your response on a separate sheet of paper.

Name ______________________________ Date ____________

Alphabetical Order

Reference materials provide facts and information about many topics. Common reference materials are dictionaries, telephone books, atlases, glossaries, encyclopedias, and thesauruses.

The information in reference materials is in **alphabetical order**. Look at the first letter of each word.

Example: apes, baboons, chimpanzees

Write each list of words in alphabetical order.

Example: fireflies, dragonflies, ladybugs
dragonflies, fireflies, ladybugs

1. Chihuahua, shepherd, Dalmatian

   ____

2. parakeet, canary, robin

   ____

3. mom, dad, sister

   ____

4. bed, sheet, lamp

   ____

5. tub, sink, water

   ____

6. numbers, letters, shapes

   ____

Write a list of words on a separate sheet of paper. Exchange papers with a classmate. Ask the classmate to write the words in alphabetical order.

Name ______________________________ Date ____________

DAILY Warm-Up 140

Alphabetical Order

Reference materials provide facts and information about many topics. Common reference materials are dictionaries, telephone books, atlases, glossaries, encyclopedias, and thesauruses.

The information in reference materials is in **alphabetical order**. When the first letter is the same, look at the next letter.

Example: because, bee, bell

PRACTICE

Write each set of words in alphabetical order.

Example: apple, ant, anchovy
anchovy, ant, apple

1. cat, catsup, can

   ____

2. dent, done, dance

   ____

3. ear, elephant, eat

   ____

4. free, friend, fresh

   ____

5. guest, goes, ghost

   ____

Write the names of three classmates. Rewrite the names in alphabetical order.

______________, ______________, ______________

______________, ______________, ______________

Name ______________________________ Date ____________

Guide Words

Reference materials provide facts and information about many topics. Common reference materials are dictionaries, telephone books, atlases, glossaries, encyclopedias, and thesauruses.

Guide words can be found at the top of each page in a reference book. The guide words tell the first and the last word on that particular page.

Example: egg–goat

Any word that begins with *e-g-g* through *g-o-a-t* will be found on this page.

Write the guide words at the top of each list of words.

Example: belt–skirt				
belt	cup	eight	boot	cloudy
coat	fork	four	cleat	dry
dress	glass	nine	cowboy	hot
jacket	knife	one	flip-flop	rainy
pajamas	mug	seven	golf	shower
pants	placemat	six	loafer	sunny
shirt	saucer	ten	sandal	warm
skirt	spoon	two	sneaker	windy

How can guide words help you to quickly find a word? Write your response on a separate sheet of paper.

Name ______________________________ Date ____________

Guide Words

Reference materials provide facts and information about many topics. Common reference materials are dictionaries, telephone books, atlases, glossaries, encyclopedias, and thesauruses.

Guide words can be found at the top of each page in a reference book. The guide words tell the first and the last word on that particular page.

Example: ring–star

Write each word under the correct set of guide words.

bison	ibis	ants	grasshopper	hyena
buffalo	horse	cougar	firefly	egret
giraffe	asp	butterfly	deer	chrysalis

anteater–cat	chimp–fly	frog–iguana
1.	1.	1.
2.	2.	2.
3.	3.	3.
4.	4.	4.
5.	5.	5.

Besides alphabetical order, in what other way could the words in a reference book be organized? Write your response on a separate sheet of paper.

Name ______________________________ Date ____________

Guide Words

Reference materials provide facts and information about many topics. Common reference materials are dictionaries, telephone books, atlases, glossaries, encyclopedias, and thesauruses.

Guide words can be found at the top of each page in a reference book. The guide words tell the first and the last word on that particular page.

Example: abacus–corner

Look up each word in a dictionary. Write the page number and the guide words for each word.

Name of dictionary: ______________________________

Word	Page	Guide Words
Example: tractor	1,324	trace–trade
1. ambulance		
2. refrigerator		
3. telephone		
4. headphones		
5. car		
6. computer		
7. ocean		
8. pebble		
9. sandwich		
10. twilight		

On a separate sheet of paper, use one of the words above correctly in a sentence.

Name ______________________________ Date ____________

DAILY Warm-Up 144

Dictionary

Reference materials provide facts and information about many topics. Common reference materials are dictionaries, telephone books, atlases, glossaries, encyclopedias, and thesauruses.

A **dictionary** is a book of words and their meanings. All of the words are listed in alphabetical order.

A dictionary can be used to find out:

- The correct spelling of the word
- The part of speech (noun, verb, etc.)
- How to say the word correctly
- The meaning of the word

Example: **couch** (cowch) *noun*, a piece of furniture to sit on.

Practice

Write the following words in alphabetical order.

television   bathrobe   very   novel   read

1. ______________________
2. ______________________
3. ______________________
4. ______________________
5. ______________________

Pick one of the words to look up in a dictionary.

Word: ______________________________

Pronunciation: ______________________________

Part of speech: ______________________________

Meaning: ______________________________

Make up a new word. On a separate sheet of paper, write a dictionary entry for the word. Share the entry with a classmate.

Name ______________________________ Date ____________

Dictionary

Reference materials provide facts and information about many topics. Common reference materials are dictionaries, telephone books, atlases, glossaries, encyclopedias, and thesauruses.

A **dictionary** is a book of words and their meanings. All of the words are listed in alphabetical order.

A dictionary can be used to find out:

- The correct spelling of the word
- How to say the word correctly
- The part of speech (noun, verb, etc.)
- The meaning of the word

Example: **read** (reed—present tense or red—past tense,) *verb*, to understand the meaning of the written word, or to say the printed words aloud

PRACTICE

Use a dictionary to find the following information about each word.

Word	Pronunciation	Part of Speech	Meaning
Ex. minute	min-it my-noot	noun adjective	a length of time equal to 60 seconds, small in size
1. school			
2. poor			
3. cool			
4. eye			
5. nap			

How do you know if a word can be pronounced two different ways? Write your response on a separate sheet of paper.

Name ______________________________ Date ____________

Dictionary

Reference materials provide facts and information about many topics. Common reference materials are dictionaries, telephone books, atlases, glossaries, encyclopedias, and thesauruses.

A **dictionary** is a book of words and their meanings. All of the words are listed in alphabetical order.

A dictionary can be used to find out:

- The correct spelling of the word
- The part of speech (noun, verb, etc.)
- How to say the word correctly
- The meaning of the word

  Example: **dog** (dawg) *noun*, a furry mammal with four legs often kept as a house pet

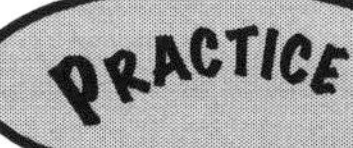

Circle the correct spelling of a word. If you need help, use a dictionary.

Example: (because)	bekause	becauze
1. haf to	have to	hafta
2. muther	mudder	mother
3. yor	yore	your
4. they	thay	thaey
5. of	uv	uve
6. leafs	leaves	leves
7. who	woh	hwo
8. frend	firend	friend
9. gril	gurl	girl
10. playd	plad	played

Is it a good idea to have a correct spelling for a given word? Why? Write your response on a separate sheet of paper.

Name ______________________________ Date ____________

Telephone Book

Reference materials provide facts and information about many topics. Common reference materials are dictionaries, telephone books, atlases, glossaries, encyclopedias, and thesauruses.

A **telephone book** lists names and businesses, their addresses, and phone numbers.

For names, the last name is listed first. The names are in alphabetical order.

Example: Johnson, Ken
Johnson, Linda and Fred
Johnson, M. and L.

PRACTICE

Use the information from the telephone book below to answer the questions.

Baker, John	1234 Garden Ave.	456–7890
Burbery, John and Mary		321–9871
Castle, Robert	988 Winchester Rd.	901–3581
Dean, Larry and Maureen	301 W. Alamo Ln., Apt. 2B	234–1567
Edwards, Kelly	10 Woodrow St., Apt. 301	540–3091
French, S. and P.	915 Locan Pkwy.	

1. Who lives on Garden Ave.? ____________
2. Which person has an unlisted address? ____________
3. Whose phone number is 901–3581? ____________
4. What is Kelly Edwards' address? ____________
5. Who lives in apartment 2B? ____________
6. What is the last name of S. and P.? ____________

On a separate sheet of paper, write your name, address, and phone number as they would be written in a phone book.

Name ______________________ Date __________

Telephone Book

Reference materials provide facts and information about many topics. Common reference materials are dictionaries, telephone books, atlases, glossaries, encyclopedias, and thesauruses.

A **telephone book** lists names and businesses, their addresses, and phone numbers.

For businesses, the names are listed in alphabetical order in categories by type of business.

Example: **Automotive Repair**

Big Al's Easy Repair	321 Herndon St.	410–3209
Casey's Garage	143 Cole Ave.	345–1876
Z.J.'s Body Shop	9032 Island Way	123–4567

PRACTICE

List each business in the correct category.

Piano Rentals	Nelson, Dr. Peter	Princeton Musical Instruments
Sports Time	Instrument Rentals	All-Season Sports Store
Khan, Dr. G.	School of Music	Johnson Medical Clinic
Team Uniforms for U	Kelsey, Dr. Samantha	Balls, Bats, and Gloves

Physicians	Sports	Instruments and Lessons
1.	1.	1.
2.	2.	2.
3.	3.	3.
4.	4.	4.

What other way could businesses be listed? Write your answer on a separate sheet of paper.

Name ______________________________ Date __________

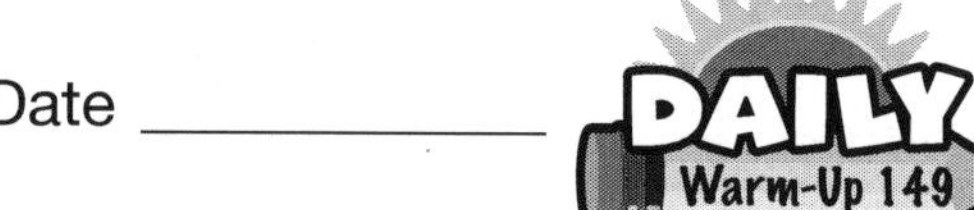

Atlas

Reference materials provide facts and information about many topics. Common reference materials are dictionaries, telephone books, atlases, glossaries, encyclopedias, and thesauruses.

An **atlas** is a book of maps. The maps show different cities, states, countries, and continents.

Name five pieces of information shown on this map.

1. ______________________________

____

2. ______________________________

____

3. ______________________________

____

4. ______________________________

____

5. ______________________________

____

How would an atlas be useful if you were traveling to another state or country? Write your response on a separate sheet of paper.

Name ______________________________ Date ____________

Encyclopedia

Reference materials provide facts and information about many topics. Common reference materials are dictionaries, telephone books, atlases, glossaries, encyclopedias, and thesauruses.

An **encyclopedia** can be one volume (book) or many volumes (books). Each volume covers several letters of the alphabet. The encyclopedia contains general information on a variety of topics. The information is listed in alphabetical order.

Example: the White House

An encyclopedia provides information about the size of the White House, who built it, when it was built, who it was built for, etc.

Sort each subject into the correct encyclopedia volume.

bee	snake	vulture	tractor	thumb
yak	dominoes	tick	Nile River	quintuplet
ukulele	robot	water	unicorn	hotel
helicopter	octopus	highway	mountain	zebra

A–Hi	Ho–Pr	Q–Th	Ti–Un	Up–Z
1.	1.	1.	1.	1.
2.	2.	2.	2.	2.
3.	3.	3.	3.	3.
4.	4.	4.	4.	4.

What is the difference between an encyclopedia and a dictionary? When would you use each reference book? Write your response on a separate sheet of paper.

Name ______________________________ Date ____________

Glossary

Reference materials provide facts and information about many topics. Common reference materials are dictionaries, telephone books, atlases, glossaries, encyclopedias, and thesauruses.

A **glossary** is a small dictionary found in the back of a book. The glossary contains special words that were used in the book. The words are in alphabetical order.

Example: amphibian: means "two lives"—frogs and toads begin their life in the water and then live on the land.

PRACTICE

Glossary

- bear: a large fur-covered mammal, with sharp claws and teeth
- cub: a baby bear
- den: a home in a cave
- fur: the outer, hairy covering on a bear or other mammal
- mammal: an animal born alive that is covered with fur, breathes with lungs, warm-blooded, and drinks milk from its mother
- omnivore: eating both plants and meat
- hibernate: to be in a deep sleep during the colder winter months

Answer the questions using the glossary above.

1. What is "a home in a cave"? ______________________
2. Name a characteristic of a mammal. ______________________
3. What does "omnivore" mean? ______________________
4. What kind of animal has fur? ______________________
5. By reading the words in the glossary, what do you think the book is about?

____

WRITE ON!

What other word(s) would you add to this glossary? Why? Write your response on a separate sheet of paper.

Name ______________________________ Date ____________

DAILY Warm-Up 152

Thesaurus

Reference materials provide facts and information about many topics. Common reference materials are dictionaries, telephone books, atlases, glossaries, encyclopedias, and thesauruses.

A **thesaurus** is a reference book. A thesaurus is a book of synonyms and antonyms. *Synonyms* are words with same or similar meanings. *Antonyms* are words with opposite meanings.

Example: educate: teach

Educate and *teach* are synonyms.

Use a thesaurus to answer the following questions.

1. Name of the thesaurus.

   ____

2. Does the thesaurus name each word's part of speech?

   ____

3. Does the thesaurus provide a definition for the word?

   ____

Use a thesaurus to find synonyms and antonyms for the following words.

Word	Synonym	Antonym
Example: bold	courageous	timid
1. go		
2. quiet		
3. new		
4. small		
5. smart		

On a separate sheet of paper, write a sentence about something that is nice. Rewrite the sentence replacing some of the words with synonyms. Which sentence is more interesting to read?

Name ______________________________ Date ____________

Dewey Decimal System

Nonfiction books contain facts and information. Many libraries use the Dewey Decimal System to arrange the nonfiction books by topic. The **Dewey Decimal System** divides the books into numbered categories.

Example: Books on spiders would be located in the 500s.

Use the Dewey Decimal System below to find out where books are located. Write down the correct Dewey Decimal number on the line.

Number	Category	Includes
000	General Works	Encyclopedias, Biographies, and Computer Science
300	Social Science	Economics, Law, Education, Customs, and Etiquette
400	Language	Dictionaries and Writing
500	Natural Science and Mathematics	Astronomy, Earth Science, Paleontology, Plants, and Animals
600	Technology and Applied Sciences	Medicine, Engineering, Agriculture, Home Economics, Manufacturing, and Building
700	Arts and Recreation	Architecture, Sculpture, Drawing, Paintings, Photography, Sports, and Performing Arts
800	Literature	Poetry, Drama, and Fiction
900	Geography and History	Travel

1. Dr. Seuss ________
2. Paragraph writing ________
3. The planets ________
4. Swimming ________
5. The continents ________
6. How to make a birdhouse ________
7. Elementary school ________
8. George Washington ________

What would you like to learn more about? Where would books on this topic be found in the library? Write your response on a separate sheet of paper.

Answer Key

Warm-Up 1 (page 8)

Person
1. artist
2. lawyer
3. gardener

Thing
1. paintbrush
2. briefcase
3. plant

Place
1. studio
2. office
3. yard

Idea
1. talent
2. power
3. joy

Warm-Up 2 (page 9)
1. thing
2. idea
3. person
4. person
5. place
6. idea
7. place
8. thing

Warm-Up 3 (page 10)

Singular Nouns
1. baby
2. brush
3. camera
4. doctor
5. farm
6. zoo

Plural Nouns
1. parks
2. beds
3. coaches
4. dads
5. schools
6. offices

Warm-Up 4 (page 11)
1. common
2. common
3. proper
4. proper
5. proper
6. common
7. proper
8. common

Check to make sure the student has used a common noun and a proper noun in the same sentence.

Warm-Up 5 (page 12)
1. faces
2. bowls
3. chairs
4. boys
5. lamps
6. doors

Warm-Up 6 (page 13)
1. many/plural
2. many/plural
3. a/singular
4. a/singular
5. one/singular
6. kinds/plural
7. six/plural
8. hundreds/plural

Warm-Up 7 (page 14)

Singular Nouns
1. man
2. woman
3. ox
4. mouse
5. person

Plural Nouns
1. mice
2. men
3. oxen
4. people
5. women

Warm-Up 8 (page 15)

Check to make sure the student has circled the following mistakes in the paragraph: childs, geese, mice, foots
1. children
2. goose
3. mouse
4. feet

Warm-Up 9 (page 16)
1. calves
2. dwarves
3. elves
4. halves
5. leaves
6. loaves
7. wives
8. wolves

Check to make sure the student has circled the following words in the sentences:
1. calfs
2. leafs
3. wolfs
4. loafs
5. wifes

Warm-Up 10 (page 17)
1. The **foxes are** always the bad guys.
2. Simon took Biggie to the **beaches**.
3. Seth broke the **glasses**.
4. I packed moving **boxes**.
5. Mina made **wishes** at the wishing well.

Warm-Up 11 (page 18)

benches, boxes, glasses, wishes
1. boxes
2. glasses
3. benches
4. wishes

Warm-Up 12 (page 19)
1. cherries
2. berries
3. ladies
4. daddies
5. candies
6. puppies
7. kitties
8. buddies
9. injuries
10. piggies
11. cities
12. families

Answer Key

Check to make sure the student has circled the following words in the paragraph: familys, citys, piggys, ladys, fairys, candys

Warm-Up 13 (page 20)

Check to make sure the student has replaced each underlined noun and helping word with a proper noun.

Sample answers:

1. Charles
2. the White House
3. Elm Street
4. Bakery Delights
5. Neptune
6. Matt
7. Fluffy
8. Toby
9. Mrs. Mayfield
10. California

Warm-Up 14 (page 21)

1. Gigantor
2. Burgers and Fries
3. Mr. Rodriguez
4. Morro Bay, California
5. Speedy-Go Scooter
6. Seattle, Washington
7. Seth Friendly
8. No-Show Eraser

Check to make sure the student has written three proper nouns for each category.

Warm-Up 15 (page 22)

Check to make sure the student has written a proper noun for each category.

Check to make sure the student has used each proper noun in a sentence.

Warm-Up 16 (page 23)

1. writes
2. sit
3. hang
4. says
5. picks
6. rings
7. hold
8. reads

Warm-Up 17 (page 24)

1. reads
2. falls
3. builds
4. practice
5. solves

Warm-Up 18 (page 25)

1. Does
2. Does
3. Do
4. Do
5. Do
6. Does
7. Does
8. Do

Warm-Up 19 (page 26)

1. is
2. are
3. are
4. is
5. are

Warm-Up 20 (page 27)

1. are
2. is
3. are
4. is
5. are
6. is

Warm-Up 21 (page 28)

1. has
2. have
3. has
4. has
5. have
6. has
7. have
8. have

Warm-Up 22 (page 29)

1. starts/present
2. looks/present
3. tasted/past
4. mopped/past
5. slipped/past
6. delivers/present

Warm-Up 23 (page 30)

1. jumped
2. washed
3. cleaned
4. baked

1. The quilt covered the bed.
2. Lino and Sal painted beautiful pictures.
3. We completed the job on time.
4. The shoes looked brand-new.

Warm-Up 24 (page 31)

1. build/built
2. hear/heard
3. freeze/froze

Answer Key

4. wear/wore
5. know/knew
6. write/wrote
7. sweep/swept
8. break/broke
9. run/ran
10. do/did
11. have/had
12. is/was

Warm-Up 25 (page 32)

1. Morgan wrote a letter.
2. Jessica swept the steps.
3. Jason did his work.
4. Victor and Thomas knew the answers.
5. Michael and George ran many laps.
6. Lena was happy.

Warm-Up 26 (page 33)

1. eat	3. sees	5. does	7. has
2. ate	4. saw	6. did	8. had

Warm-Up 27 (page 34)

1. Lindsay and I/We
2. Mom/She
3. Gracie/She
4. The dessert/It
5. David/He
6. The stars/They

Warm-Up 28 (page 35)

1. Nathaniel/He
2. Mrs. Torres/She
3. Ariana and I/We
4. Mr. Montez/He
5. Seth and Clem/They
6. Buster/It

Warm-Up 29 (page 36)

Subject Pronouns

1. it	3. I	5. they
2. we	4. you	

Nouns

1. Dwight	4. Mrs. Rogers
2. Grandma	5. Chip and Tip
3. Buster	

Verbs

1. reads	4. works
2. talks	5. washes
3. sleeps	

Warm-Up 30 (page 37)

1. noun	5. noun
2. verb	6. verb
3. verb	7. noun
4. subject pronoun	8. subject pronoun

Warm-Up 31 (page 38)

1. Mary Jane	6. reads
2. sawed	7. They
3. We	8. beach
4. television	9. sings
5. She	10. clapped

Warm-Up 32 (page 39)

Check to make sure the student has circled the following sentences: 3, 4, 5, 8, 10

Warm-Up 33 (page 40)

1. went to her grandma's house
2. David
3. sailed into the harbor
4. Michelle
5. graduated today
6. played football
7. the president
8. surfed all day

Warm-Up 34 (page 41)

Check to make sure the student has completed each sentence.

Warm-Up 35 (page 42)

Check to make sure the student has written a complete sentence about each picture.

Warm-Up 36 (page 43)

Check to make sure the student has circled the following sentences: 2, 3, 5, 6

Check to make sure the student has written a declarative sentence about the picture.

Warm-Up 37 (page 44)

Check to make sure the student has written a complete sentence that answers each question.

Answer Key

Check to make sure the student has written a sentence about and drawn a picture of a pet he or she would like to have.

Warm-Up 38 (page 45)

1. Cassie does play the violin.
2. Brent has washed the car.
3. Jason is feeding the dog.
4. They are here.

Carla is painting a picture.

Warm-Up 39 (page 46)

Check to make sure the student has added question marks to the following sentences: 1, 4, 5, 6, 8

Check to make sure the student has written a question about the picture.

Warm-Up 40 (page 47)

1. Does the telephone ring at odd times?
2. Can Marcus bowl a perfect game?
3. Did Wanda get sick from eating candy?
4. Was the house haunted?

Check to make sure the student has written a question about the picture.

Warm-Up 41 (page 48)

Check to make sure the student has written a question about each picture.

Warm-Up 42 (page 49)

Check to make sure the student has circled the following sentences: 2, 3, 4, 6, 7, 9

Check to make sure the student has written an imperative sentence.

Warm-Up 43 (page 50)

Check to make sure the student has rewritten each sentence as an imperative sentence.

Sample answers:

1. Do your homework.
2. Make your bed.
3. Put on a sweater when it is cold outside.
4. Use the crosswalk.
5. Button your jacket.
6. Cut your hair.

Warm-Up 44 (page 51)

Check to make sure the student has written an imperative sentence for each picture.

Warm-Up 45 (page 52)

Check to make sure the student has added an exclamation point to the following sentences: 2, 4, 5, 7, 8

Check to make sure the student has written an exclamatory sentence about the picture.

Warm-Up 46 (page 53)

Story #1

He won!

Story #2

How exciting!

Check to make sure the student has written an exclamatory sentence about the picture.

Warm-Up 47 (page 54)

Check to make sure the student has written an exclamatory sentence about each picture.

Warm-Up 48 (page 55)

1. I
2. E
3. I
4. IM
5. D
6. E

Warm-Up 49 (page 56)

1. Where is Marvin?
2. The pancakes are delicious.
3. Johnny loves to sing.
4. When is the test?
5. Can you help me?
6. We played in the tree house.
7. You need to make your bed.
8. The bakery is open.

Warm-Up 50 (page 57)

1. The apples are juicy.
2. Mr. Radford has a new pet.
3. Molly makes wonderful spaghetti.
4. The kids are in the pool.
5. Kathleen needs help.
6. Daisy walked on the beach.

Warm-Up 51 (page 58)

Check to make sure the student has completed the chart and has written a paragraph telling how the house cat and tiger are the same.

Answer Key

Warm-Up 52 (page 59)
Check to make sure the student has completed the chart and has written a paragraph telling how the house cat and tiger are different.

Warm-Up 53 (page 60)
Check to make sure the student has completed the Venn diagram.

Warm-Up 54 (page 61)
1. April 15, 2005
2. June 5, 2008
3. August 16, 2009
4. February 9, 2000
5. December 20, 2003
6. July 31, 2007
7. January 30, 2001
8. September 1, 2004

Check to make sure the student has completed each date.

Warm-Up 55 (page 62)
1. Hello Dad,
2. Hi Tom,
3. To Mr. and Mrs. Smith,
4. Hello Dana,

Check to make sure the student has written each greeting correctly.

Warm-Up 56 (page 63)
Check to make sure the student has written three questions and three statements.

Warm-Up 57 (page 64)
1. Your best friend,
   Taylor
2. See you soon,
   Ana
3. Hugs and kisses,
   Chad
4. Love always,
   Reed
5. Sincerely yours,
   Tamra
6. Love,
   Arnie

Warm-Up 58 (page 65)
A. Date
B. Greeting
C. Body
D. Closing
E. Signature

Warm-Up 59 (page 66)
Check to make sure the student has written a friendly letter using the correct letter format.

Warm-Up 60 (page 67)
Letter #1
The greeting

Letter #2
The body of the letter

Warm-Up 61 (page 68)

1. cap	5. mop
2. tub	6. pen
3. bed	7. bat
4. pig	8. mug

Warm-Up 62 (page 69)
1. teeth
2. fish
3. sock
4. whistle
5. dish
6. thorn
7. chin
8. ship

Warm-Up 63 (page 70)

1. robe	7. nape
2. made	8. mate
3. cope	9. bite
4. mope	10. time
5. cape	11. rate
6. pine	12. pane

1. dims/dimes	5. not/note
2. pin/pine	6. man/mane
3. cans/canes	7. fin/fine
4. tub/tube	8. hop/hope

Answer Key

Warm-Up 64 (page 71)

EA Words

1. neat
2. mean
3. bean
4. steam

EE Words

1. meet
2. teen
3. feel
4. seeds

1. bean
2. meet
3. seeds
4. mean

Warm-Up 65 (page 72)

1. stop
2. stand
3. slot
4. cramp
5. lost
6. clasp
7. soft
8. belt

Check to make sure the student has written two words with consonant blends.

Warm-Up 66 (page 73)

–K Words

1. ask
2. bunk
3. chunk
4. park
5. silk

–CK Words

1. sack
2. pack
3. sick
4. sock
5. peck

–IC Words

1. music
2. magic
3. plastic
4. magnetic
5. Titanic

Warm-Up 67 (page 74)

1. soil
2. point
3. noise
4. coin
5. oil
6. voice
7. foil
8. boil

Warm-Up 68 (page 75)

1. boy
2. destroy
3. oyster
4. voyage
5. enjoy
6. royal

Warm-Up 69 (page 76)

1. Our
2. cloud
3. outdoors
4. found
5. count
6. hour

Warm-Up 70 (page 77)

AR Words

1. are
2. card
3. party
4. army
5. yard

ER Words

1. were
2. her
3. over
4. ever
5. mother

IR Words

1. circle
2. shirt
3. birthday
4. girl
5. first

OR Words

1. more
2. important
3. store
4. born
5. before

Warm-Up 71 (page 78)

1. stars
2. forget
3. sister
4. better
5. arm
6. third
7. bakery
8. afternoon

Check to make sure the student has written four words with *r*-controlled vowels.

Answer Key

Warm-Up 72 (page 79)

1. ovr/over
2. sae/say *or* sae/save
3. tri/try
4. nu/new
5. grate/great
6. Whare/Where
7. ind/end
8. sa/saw
9. muve/move
10. gud/good
11. nead/need
12. bcause/because
13. larj/large
14. bak/back

Warm-Up 73 (page 80)

Check to make sure the student has circled the following words in the story: Peple, luk, sam, bigg, rit, thre, gril, yu

1. People	5. right
2. look	6. three
3. same	7. girl
4. big	8. you

Warm-Up 74 (page 81)

1. know	5. knows
2. No	6. no
3. knows	7. knows
4. no	8. no

Warm-Up 75 (page 82)

1. to	5. two
2. too	6. too
3. two	7. too
4. to	8. two

Warm-Up 76 (page 83)

1. Our	5. hour
2. are	6. Our
3. hours	7. are
4. our	8. hour

Warm-Up 77 (page 84)

1. ate	3. eight	5. ate	7. ate
2. eight	4. eight	6. eight	8. ate

Warm-Up 78 (page 85)

1. there	4. There
2. their	5. Their
3. They're	6. They're

Warm-Up 79 (page 86)

1. and	5. an
2. a	6. a
3. An	7. and
4. a	8. a

Warm-Up 80 (page 87)

1. much	3. many	5. much
2. many	4. many	6. much

Warm-Up 81 (page 88)

1. twins', twinkle, twine
2. Marvelous, Mary, makes, maple, mother's
3. Sally Summers, sometimes, sits, sun, smelling sunflowers
4. Dean Davis, dad, Derek, do, double, duty, during, demolition, derby
5. Jay, journeys, jet, gerbil, Jerome
6. Bill's, baby, blanket, barely, bed
7. Kelly, cousin, Kim, canned, cucumbers, carrots
8. Charles, chunky, chocolate, chip, cheer, Chuck

Check to make sure the student has written three words that have the same beginning sound as each word.

Warm-Up 82 (page 89)

Check to make sure the student has completed the Alliteration activity page.

Warm-Up 83 (page 90)

Check to make sure the student has circled the following words:

1. car, star, scar
2. fancy, Nancy, antsy
3. solar, polar, molar
4. hairy, fairy, Jerry
5. calf, laugh, half
6. head, bed, fed
7. cake, rake, shake
8. pipe, stripe, type

Check to make sure the student has written three rhyming words for each word.

Answer Key

Warm-Up 84 (page 91)

1. banana
2. wall
3. fault
4. puppy
5. winner
6. bone
7. late
8. bear

Warm-Up 85 (page 92)

1. child/ E. youngster
2. eyeglasses/ J. spectacles
3. hat/ A. bonnet
4. number/ G. digit
5. jeans/ C. pants
6. mutt/ I. dog
7. picture/ B. photograph
8. shirt/ D. top
9. sofa/ F. couch
10. tree/ H. plant

Check to make sure the student has written a synonym for each word.

Warm-Up 86 (page 93)

1. error, mistake
2. add, total
3. globe, world
4. tiny, small
5. unmoving, still
6. try, attempt
7. hurts, pain
8. last, end
9. enormous, large
10. may, might
11. noise, loud
12. fresh, new
13. see, looking
14. listen, hear

Warm-Up 87 (page 94)

1. brother/ J. sister
2. closed/ G. open
3. dark/ E. light
4. dog/ A. cat
5. early/ D. late
6. happy/ I. sad
7. love/ C. hate
8. mom/ B. dad
9. on/ F. off
10. salt/ H. pepper

Check to make sure the student has rewritten each sentence.

Warm-Up 88 (page 95)

1. big, little
2. hard, soft
3. hot, cold
4. hill, valley
5. up, down
6. buy, sell
7. boys, girls
8. together, alone
9. bent, straighten
10. none, all
11. repaired, broken
12. clean, dirty
13. heel, toe
14. tiny, huge

Warm-Up 89 (page 96)

1. S	3. S	5. S
2. A	4. A	6. A

Warm-Up 90 (page 97)

Check to make sure the student has written the meaning of each compound word.

Sample answers:

1. campfire: a fire at a camp
2. buttermilk: milk from butter
3. clothesline: a line for hanging clothes
4. goldfish: fish that is gold in color
5. crosswalk: a walkway for crossing the street
6. shoelace: a lace for shoes

1. pancake
2. haystack
3. pigtail

Answer Key

Warm-Up 91 (page 98)

1. skateboard
2. rowboat
3. cupcake
4. eyeball
5. fireplace
6. earthquake
7. newspaper
8. football

Warm-Up 92 (page 99)

Check to make sure the student has made a list of compound words.

Sample answers: airman, airway, handball, ballroom, outboard, boardroom, boardwalk, doorman, outdoor, doorway, grandmother, handshake, spaceman, steamroom, spacewalk

Warm-Up 93 (page 100)

Check to make sure the student has circled the following words: bathrobe, necklace, overalls, raincoat, shoelace, swimsuit, turtleneck, wristwatch

Check to make sure the student has written each compound word as well as its meaning.

Sample answers:

1. bathrobe: a robe to wear after taking a bath
2. necklace: lace or jewelry worn around the neck
3. overalls: clothing that covers all of the body
4. raincoat: coat for wearing in the rain
5. shoelace: a lace for a shoe
6. swimsuit: a suit for swimming in
7. turtleneck: a shirt that covers the entire neck
8. wristwatch: a watch worn around the wrist

Warm-Up 94 (page 101)

1. 1	9. 3
2. 2	10. 2
3. 2	11. 1
4. 2	12. 2
5. 1	13. 1
6. 1	14. 2
7. 2	15. 3
8. 2	

Check to make sure the student has written each word.

Warm-Up 95 (page 102)

Long Vowels	Short Vowels
1. ba/by	1. cab/in
2. ba/ker	2. den/im
3. u/nite	3. riv/er
4. pho/to	4. grav/el
5. na/vy	5. lem/on
6. ti/ger	6. liz/ard

Warm-Up 96 (page 103)

1. arto	car/ton
2. iste	mis/ter
3. utto	but/ton
4. atte	pat/tern
5. umpe	trum/pet
6. otto	bot/tom
7. ictu	pic/ture
8. enni	ten/nis
9. allo	shal/low
10. iffe	dif/fer
11. ibbo	rib/bon
12. anke	blan/ket
13. izza	piz/za
14. ette	bet/ter
15. illo	pil/low
16. irro	mir/ror
17. inno	min/now
18. aske	bas/ket

Check to make sure the student has written two words that fit the VCCV pattern.

Warm-Up 97 (page 104)

1. ex/plain	1. Eng/lish
2. im/prove	2. hun/gry
3. hun/dred	3. dis/trust
4. part/ner	4. por/tray
5. con/stant	5. ex/tra
6. dol/phin	6. pump/kin
7. em/ploy	7. in/stead
8. mon/ster	8. sub/tract

Answer Key

Warm-Up 98 (page 105)

1. bath/room
2. Sun/day
3. hair/cut
4. paint/brush
5. back/pack
6. light/house
7. trash/can
8. in/to
9. rose/bud
10. cup/cake
11. pan/cake
12. sweat/shirt
13. car/wash
14. head/ache
15. pea/nut
16. hop/scotch
17. eye/ball
18. neck/lace
19. shoe/lace
20. flash/light

Warm-Up 99 (page 106)

Prefixes

1. re/tell
2. pre/heat
3. sub/title
4. un/like
5. over/eat

Suffixes

1. friend/ly
2. teach/er
3. play/ing
4. meat/less
5. joy/ful

Warm-Up 100 (page 107)

1. unsafe
2. dislike
3. retell
4. disable or unable
5. reread
6. uneaten
7. disorder
8. recover

1. unable
2. recover
3. dislike

Warm-Up 101 (page 108)

1. overpay—pay too much
2. subzero—below zero
3. preschool—before kindergarten
4. overeat—eat too much
5. pregame—before the actual game
6. subnormal—below normal
7. overact—act too much
8. prewash—to wash before

1. preschool
2. overeat
3. prewash

Warm-Up 102 (page 109)

1. teacher
2. readable
3. helpful
4. wearable
5. swimmer
6. drinkable
7. useful
8. beautiful

1. beautiful
2. teacher
3. swimmer

Warm-Up 103 (page 110)

Check to make sure the student has made a list of words using each base word and suffix.

Sample words: friendless, friendly, helping, helpless, hoping, hopeless, meatless, slowing, slowly

1. meatless
2. slowing
3. friendly

Answer Key

Warm-Up 104 (page 111)

box: a cube-shaped container, a sport

bowl: a sport with balls and pins, a round dish

can: to be able to, a metal or aluminum container

ear: something to hear with, a corn cob

foot: a body part, twelve inches in length

pupil: a student, the inner part of one's eye

shower: a light rain, used to clean oneself

staple: metal to fasten papers together, a standard food item

tie: to fasten items together, an item worn around a man's neck

wave: moving a hand back and forth, the cresting water in the ocean

1. a student
2. a light rain
3. to fasten the laces on shoes

Warm-Up 105 (page 112)

1. grade
2. copy
3. fit
4. diamond
5. fall
6. dress
7. land
8. cry
9. baby
10. eye

Warm-Up 106 (page 113)

1. the leader of a country, to stack two checkers together
2. to move back and forth in a chair, a stone
3. a game children play, a sticker with the price of an item
4. a person hitting a ball, a mixture used to make a cake or brownies
5. to teach an animal tricks, a vehicle that moves on tracks

Warm-Up 107 (page 114)

1. noun
2. verb
3. verb
4. noun
5. verb
6. noun
7. noun
8. verb
9. verb
10. noun

Warm-Up 108 (page 115)

1. Thomas knows how to add, subtract, multiply, and divide.
2. Michaela likes to collect toys, dolls, bears, and rocks.
3. Gretchen planted roses, petunias, tulips, and lilies.
4. Teddy packed pants, shorts, socks, and belts.

Warm-Up 109 (page 116)

1. Trisha has a television, radio, and video games.
4. Anissa was wearing earrings, bracelets, necklaces, and rings.

Warm-Up 110 (page 117)

Story #1

The students wanted to have cupcakes, cookies, punch, and party bags.

The students would also need plates, cups, and napkins.

Story #2

Our school colors are red, white, and black.

We have a football team, a softball team, and a basketball team.

We also have craft classes like painting, ceramics, photography, and scrapbooking.

Story #3

There were rolls, turkey, cranberry sauce, stuffing, and potatoes.

For dessert there were pies, cakes, candies, and ice cream.

Warm-Up 111 (page 118)

1. <u>I am going to use my grandma's secret recipe</u>
3. <u>Yum!</u>
6. <u>May I have your recipe, Mrs. Simpson?</u>
7. <u>Certainly</u>

Warm-Up 112 (page 119)

1. "Where do you live?"
2. "I found my lucky penny!"
3. "I forgot what I was going to say!"
4. "When is recess?"
5. "Wow! Look at that tall tree!"
6. "Are Rich and Patrick twins?"
7. "Where did I put my soccer bag?"
8. "Can we go skiing this weekend?"
9. "Which shape do you like best?"
10. "My favorite season is fall,"

Answer Key

Warm-Up 113 (page 120)

1. "When I get home," said Dad, "we can go roller skating."
2. "Well, the window was open," said the student, "and a woodpecker came flying into the room."
3. "Here comes the mail carrier," said Stewart, "and she's carrying a big package!"
4. "In case of an emergency," said the police officer, "remember to dial 9-1-1."

1. "What do you want to be when you grow up?" asked Samantha.
2. "After school," said Elijah, "let's go to the snack bar."

Warm-Up 114 (page 121)
Paragraph #1

"It's snowing!" screamed Ralph. "Let's make a snow family!"

"Okay!" said Wanda. "I'll grab carrots for the noses and some raisins for the eyes."

"They look great," said Wanda.

"It was a lot of fun," said Ralph.

Paragraph #2

"Oh, no," sighed Wanda, "the family is melting!"

"Don't worry," said Ralph, "the next time it snows, we can make another family."

"I will save these for the next family we make," said Wanda.

"Good idea," said Ralph.

Warm-Up 115 (page 122)

1. Christian's airplane
2. Gabriel's jacket
3. brother's backpack
4. Reanna's eyeglasses
5. Mom's car
6. Sam's movie
7. Audrey's hair
8. Grandma's lamp

1. Frank's
2. lamp's
3. dog's
4. Martin's

Warm-Up 116 (page 123)
Story #1

Stacy's, lady's, Mom's

Story #2

Dad's, Dad's, kids'

Warm-Up 117 (page 124)

1. soldiers' boots
2. scouts' uniforms
3. flags' stripes
4. swans' feathers
5. cats' paws
6. trees' fruit

1. reporters'
2. stores'
3. peacocks'
4. dogs'
5. students'

Warm-Up 118 (page 125)

1. I'll
2. he's
3. we're
4. that's
5. you've
6. I'm
7. don't
8. won't
9. haven't
10. isn't

1. is not/isn't
2. Do not/Don't
3. He is/ He's
4. That is/That's

Warm-Up 119 (page 126)

1. you're
2. she's
3. it's
4. you'll
5. they're
6. I've
7. won't
8. couldn't
9. she'll
10. we're

1. You're/You are
2. couldn't/could not
3. isn't/is not
4. It's/It is

Answer Key

Warm-Up 120 (page 127)
1. I'm
2. It's
3. I'll
4. I've
5. they'll

Warm-Up 121 (page 128)
1. Roeding Zoo
2. Zippo Sneakers
3. Elm Lane
4. Stella

Check to make sure the student has written a proper noun for each category.

Warm-Up 122 (page 129)

Person
1. Dr. Morris
2. Ms. Nolan
3. Mr. Simmons
4. Riley
5. Principal Rogers

Place
1. Pancake Barn
2. White House
3. Sandy Beach
4. Fresno Zoo
5. Burger Time

Thing
1. Speedy Shoes
2. Spot
3. Puffy Bikes
4. Cube-It Blocks
5. Shiny Shampoo

Warm-Up 123 (page 130)
Check to make sure the student has drawn three lines under the capital letter(s) in each sentence.

Warm-Up 124 (page 131)
1. My family and I go camping.
2. We take along tents and sleeping bags.
3. My mom packs the food.
4. My dad takes us on hikes.
5. My brother loves to canoe.
6. At night we roast marshmallows.

Warm-Up 125 (page 132)
1. February
2. June
3. April
4. May
5. September
6. August

1. Sara has a birthday in December.
2. In October, Alice turns fifty-nine.
3. The final hockey game is in January.
4. Were you born in March?
5. There are thirty-one days in July.

Warm-Up 126 (page 133)
1. Thursday
2. Wednesday
3. Tuesday
4. Monday
5. Sunday
6. Friday

1. I have a piano lesson on Tuesday.
2. Every Friday night is family game night.
3. Do you have karate practice on Monday?
4. Is the library open on Wednesday?

Warm-Up 127 (page 134)
Check to make sure the student has circled the following sentences:
1. The math class is taught by Professor Manning.
2. Where is Detective Johnson?
3. Nurse Adams is on the third floor.
4. Principal Hensel loves to work with children.

1. I take my pets to see Doctor Warner.
2. Judge Holt is a very fair person.
3. Mayor Streets always keeps her word.

Warm-Up 128 (page 135)
1. My initials are M.C.R.
2. Have you eaten at C.J.'s Barbecue?
3. M.B. threw the winning pitch.
4. You can call me Benny Bean or B.B. for short.
5. Uncle J.R. lives in Kansas.
6. My mom loves the poems by C. C. Edgemont.

Answer Key

Warm-Up 129 (page 136)

1. Hanukkah
2. Thanksgiving
3. Yom Kippur
4. Ramadan
5. Mother's Day
6. New Year's Day
7. Christmas
8. Veteran's Day

1. Groundhog Day
2. Valentine's Day
3. Lincoln's Birthday
4. President's Day

Warm-Up 130 (page 137)

Check to make sure the student has underlined the following titles:

1. <u>Speedy to the Rescue</u>
2. <u>Dancing Roses</u>
3. <u>Even You Can Learn to Tap Dance</u>
4. <u>Learn to Type in Ten Easy Lessons</u>
5. <u>Camels Come to Dinner</u>
6. <u>The World's Funniest Videos</u>
7. <u>Boys in Toyland</u>
8. <u>Cooking with Shmo and Joe</u>

Check to make sure the student has written a title of a favorite book and a title of a favorite movie with correct capitalization and punctuation.

Warm-Up 131 (page 138)

1. Doctor/Dr.
2. Professor/Prof.
3. Sergeant/Sgt.
4. Captain/Capt.
5. Junior/Jr.
6. Senior/Sr.
7. Superintendent/Supt.
8. President/Pres.

1. Fred Jr. is named after his dad, Fred Sr.
2. Supt. Jones runs the school district.
3. Capt. Parisi has sailed ships for many years.

Warm-Up 132 (page 139)

1. Hwy.	6. St.
2. Ct.	7. Ln.
3. Ave.	8. E.
4. N.	9. Tpk.
5. mi.	10. S.

Warm-Up 133 (page 140)

1. AR	5. ID	9. NE	13. UT
2. CO	6. IL	10. OH	14. WA
3. DE	7. IN	11. OK	15. WI
4. FL	8. MA	12. OR	16. WY

1. Seattle, WA
2. Boston, MA
3. Orlando, FL
4. Denver, CO

Warm-Up 134 (page 141)

1. Arizona/AZ
2. Connecticut/CT
3. Georgia/GA
4. Hawaii/HI
5. Kansas/KS
6. Kentucky/KY
7. Louisiana/LA
8. Maine/ME
9. Maryland/MD
10. Montana/MT
11. Nevada/NV
12. Tennessee/TN
13. Texas/TX
14. Vermont/VT
15. Virginia/VA

Warm-Up 135 (page 142)

1. NJ	3. NC	5. RI	7. SD
2. NY	4. ND	6. SC	8. WV

Check to make sure the student has circled the following words: New Mexico, New Hampshire, North Carolina, South Carolina, West Virginia, Rhode Island

1. NM	4. SC
2. NH	5. WV
3. NC	6. RI

Answer Key

Warm-Up 136 (page 143)

1. Saturday
2. Monday
3. Friday
4. Thursday
5. Tuesday
6. Wednesday

Check to make sure the student has circled the following words: Monday, Wednesday, Tuesday, Thursday, Saturday, Sunday, Friday

1. Mon.
2. Wed.
3. Tues.
4. Thur.
5. Sat.
6. Sun.
7. Fri.

Warm-Up 137 (page 144)

1. Oct.
2. Mar.
3. Feb.
4. May
5. Apr.

Check to make sure the student has answered each question using abbreviations.

Warm-Up 138 (page 145)

1. tbsp.
2. mi.
3. c.
4. oz.
5. qt.
6. yd.
7. tsp.
8. pt.
9. lb.
10. gal.

Warm-Up 139 (page 146)

1. Chihuahua, Dalmatian, shepherd
2. canary, parakeet, robin
3. dad, mom, sister
4. bed, lamp, sheet
5. sink, tub, water
6. letters, numbers, shapes

Warm-Up 140 (page 147)

1. can, cat, catsup
2. dance, dent, done
3. ear, eat, elephant
4. free, fresh, friend
5. ghost, goes, guest

Warm-Up 141 (page 148)

cup—spoon
eight—two
boot—sneaker
cloudy—windy

Warm-Up 142 (page 149)

anteater–cat

1. bison
2. buffalo
3. asp
4. ants
5. butterfly

chimp–fly

1. cougar
2. firefly
3. deer
4. egret
5. chrysalis

frog–iguana

1. giraffe
2. ibis
3. horse
4. grasshopper
5. hyena

Warm-Up 143 (page 150)

Check to make sure the student has completed the Guide Words activity page.

Warm-Up 144 (page 151)

1. bathrobe
2. novel
3. read
4. television
5. very

Check to make sure the student has looked up one of the words in a dictionary and has answered the questions.

Answer Key

Warm-Up 145 (page 152)
Check to make sure the student has completed the dictionary activity page.

Warm-Up 146 (page 153)
1. have to
2. mother
3. your
4. they
5. of
6. leaves
7. who
8. friend
9. girl
10. played

Warm-Up 147 (page 154)
1. John Baker
2. John and Mary Burbery
3. Robert Castle
4. 10 Woodrow St., Apt. 301
5. Larry and Maureen Dean
6. French

Warm-Up 148 (page 155)
Physicians
1. Khan, Dr. G.
2. Nelson, Dr. Peter
3. Kelsey, Dr. Samantha
4. Johnson Medical Clinic

Sports
1. Sports Time
2. Team Uniforms for U
3. All-Season Sports Store
4. Balls, Bats, and Gloves

Instruments and Lessons
1. Piano Rentals
2. Instrument Rentals
3. School of Music
4. Princeton Musical Instruments

Warm-Up 149 (page 156)
Check to make sure the student has named five pieces of information shown on the map.

Sample answers:
1. Names of neighboring state (Nevada)
2. Name of ocean (Pacific Ocean)
3. Name of river (Sacramento River)
4. Name of mountain range (Sierra Nevada Mountains)
5. Names of major cities (i.e., Sacramento)

Warm-Up 150 (page 157)

A–Hi
bee
helicopter
dominoes
highway

Ho–Pr
octopus
Nile River
mountain
hotel

Q–Th
snake
robot
thumb
quintuplet

Ti–Un
ukulele
tick
tractor
unicorn

Up–Z
yak
vulture
water
zebra

Warm-Up 151 (page 158)
1. den
2. Answers will vary.
3. eating both plants and meat
4. bear or other mammal
5. bears

Warm-Up 152 (page 159)
Check to make sure the student has completed the Thesaurus activity page.
Sample answers:
1. go/move/stay
2. quiet/peaceful/noisy
3. new/fresh/old
4. small/little/large
5. smart/intelligent/dull

Warm-Up 153 (page 160)

1. 800	3. 500	5. 900	7. 300
2. 400	4. 700	6. 600	8. 000

Name ______________________________ Date __________

Verbs

A **verb** is the action word in a sentence. A verb tells what somebody or something does.

Example: The cars stop at the red light.
Stop is the verb. It tells what the cars did.

Underline the verb in each sentence.

Example: The girl kicks the soccer ball.

1. Mr. Figura writes on the chalkboard.
2. The children sit at their desks.
3. The students hang up their coats.
4. The class says the flag salute.
5. Coco picks up the students.
6. The bell rings to start class.
7. The backpacks hold all the books.
8. Mrs. McKinney reads the lunch menu.

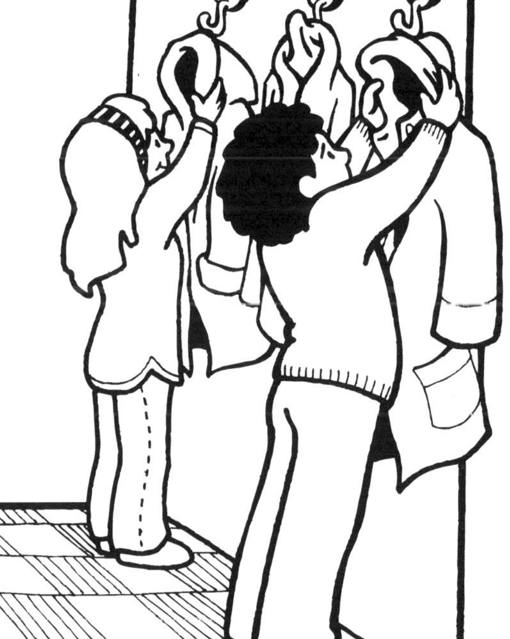

Write about what you did yesterday on a separate sheet of paper. Use a verb in each sentence, and underline it.

Name ________________________________ Date ____________

DAILY Warm-Up 17

Verbs

A **verb** is the action word in a sentence. A verb tells what somebody or something does.

- A **singular verb** goes with a singular subject. A singular verb ends in *–s*.
  Example: Camille rides her bike every day.
- A **plural verb** goes with a plural subject. A plural verb does not end in *–s*.
  Example: Clay and Camille ride their bikes every day.

Complete each sentence with the correct form of the verb.

Example: Marisol <u>folds</u> the clothes.
fold folds

1. Sam ________________ the newspaper each day.
   read reads
2. The rain ________________ down from the clouds.
   fall falls
3. Wendy ________________ towers with the blocks.
   build builds
4. Ben and Liz ________________ their instruments after school.
   practice practices

5. The robot ________________ problems in the blink of an eye.
   solve solves

On a separate sheet of paper, use the singular form and the plural form of the same verb in a pair of sentences. Underline the verb in each sentence.

Name ______________________________ Date ____________

Helping Verbs

A **verb** is the action word in a sentence. A verb tells what somebody or something does.

Do and *does* are helping verbs. A **helping verb** has no meaning by itself in a sentence. A helping verb connects information about the subject to the subject. The verb *do* is often used to ask a question.

- Use *does* with singular subjects.
  Example: Does Mabel cook all of the food?
- Use *do* with plural subjects.
  Example: Do Mabel and Santiago cook all of the food?

Singular Nouns		Plural Nouns	
Do	I	Do	we
Do	you	Do	you
Does	he, she, it	Do	they

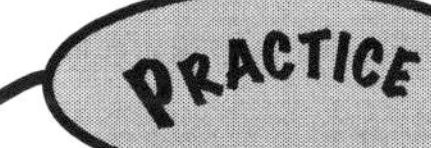

Complete each question with the correct form of the *do* verb.

Example: Do you like yard sales?

1. ________ your dog bite?
2. ________ Emma know the answer?
3. ________ they like the movie?
4. ________ we turn left at the light?
5. ________ you belong to the gym?
6. ________ Dr. Taylor have the files?
7. ________ the dress fit?
8. ________ they plan on coming to the play?

WRITE ON!

On a separate sheet of paper, ask two questions. Use *does* in one question and *do* in the second question.

Name ______________________________ Date ____________

Helping Verbs

A **verb** is the action word in a sentence. A verb tells what somebody or something does.

Is and *are* are helping verbs. A **helping verb** has no meaning by itself in a sentence. A helping verb connects information about the subject to the subject.

- Use *is* with singular subjects.
  Example: Bella is happy.
- Use *are* with plural subjects.
  Example: Bella and Ruben are happy.

Use *is* or *are* to complete each sentence.

Example: The ticket booth _is_ open.

1. The caboose ______ the last car of the train.
2. Some of the cars ______ for sleeping.
3. Train tickets ______ cheaper than plane tickets.
4. Our class ______ going to go on a train ride.
5. Trains ______ fun to ride on.

On a separate sheet of paper, write about traveling by train. Use the helping verbs *is* and *are* in the story, and underline them.

Name ____________________________________ Date ____________

Helping Verbs

A **verb** is the action word in a sentence. A verb tells what somebody or something does.

- *Is* is a **singular helping verb**. *Is* is used with a subject that names one person, place, thing, or idea.

  Example: Jose is a good student.

- *Are* is a **plural helping verb**. *Are* is used with a subject that names more than one person, place, thing, or idea.

  Example: Jose and Anna are good students.

Singular	Plural
I am	We are
You are	You are
He is She is It is	They are

- *Are* can also be a **singular helping verb**. *Are* is used with the singular subject *you*.

  Example: You are a good student.

Complete each sentence with the correct helping verb.

Example: Perry __is__ working on the car.

1. Dr. Hall and Dr. Troy ______ the best dentists in town.
2. The toy car ______ for you.
3. Clara, May, and Nicky ______ in the same class.
4. The picture ______ crooked.
5. My dog and I ______ playing fetch.
6. The phone ______ ringing.

On a separate sheet of paper, write two sentences using the word *is* and two sentences using the word *are*.

Name ______________________________ Date ____________

Helping Verbs

A **verb** is the action word in a sentence. A verb tells what somebody or something does.

Has and *have* are helping verbs. A **helping verb** has no meaning by itself in a sentence. A helping verb connects information about the subject to the subject.

- Use *has* with singular subjects.
  Example: Tom has many marbles.
- Use *have* with plural subjects.
  Example: Tom and Fritz have many marbles.

PRACTICE

Use *has* or *have* to complete each sentence.

Example: Mrs. Moore <u>has</u> a new granddaughter.

1. The ball ______________ many stripes.
2. Neil and his brother ______________ the latest set of trading cards.
3. Minerva ______________ fifty cents.
4. Channel 26 ______________ the latest news and weather.
5. Maya and Sierra ______________ a big collection of dolls.
6. The punch ______________ ten kinds of fruit in it.
7. They ______________ collected the most cans for the recycling drive.
8. We ______________ a fire drill every month.

On a separate sheet of paper, write about a fire drill. Use the verbs *has* and *have* in the sentences, and underline them.